THE
SPIRIT
OF THE
LORD
IS UPON
US

DISCOVERING THE ANOINTING TO SHARE THE
GOSPEL, SET PEOPLE FREE, AND EXPERIENCE
THE SUPERNATURAL IN YOUR LIFE

"THE SPIRIT OF THE LORD IS UPON ME,

BECAUSE HE ANOINTED ME TO PREACH

THE GOSPEL TO THE POOR.

HE HAS SENT ME TO PROCLAIM

RELEASE TO THE CAPTIVES,

AND RECOVERY OF SIGHT TO THE BLIND,

TO SET FREE THOSE WHO ARE OPPRESSED."

LUKE 4:18 (NASB)

What People Are Saying About[1]

The Spirit of the Lord is Upon Us

"I highly recommend this life-changing resource to all who seek a deeper and more powerful life of ministry that will help to transform our world for Christ."

Glenn C. Burris, Jr.
President, The Foursquare Church

"It is a faith-inspiring book, theologically sound, with profound implications on how Christians can live as 'Kingdom-agents' in this world. You will be thrilled by the testimonies of exciting miracles happening in our days."

Volker Heitz
Chairman, Foursquare Europe
National Leader, Foursquare Suisse

---

[1] To read the full endorsements, go to www.foursquaremissionspress.org/keegel

"This book shares the whole counsel of the gospel of Christ in a way that we can apply to our daily walk with the Lord. It is a book that will mentor you to walk in the love, grace, compassion, and the power of the gospel of Jesus Christ."

Rajan Thiagarajah
Founder/Pastor, Good Success Church

"The Spirit of the Lord is Upon Us is an absolute must-read for anyone longing to step into the power of the Holy Spirit. Dr. Leslie Keegel humbly shares his incredible journey into a miracle-filled ministry, straight out of the book of Acts."

Jerry M. Stott
South Pacific Foursquare

"His personal stories of life and ministry in Sri Lanka and throughout the nations will remind you that the Holy Spirit is alive and well, moving in power through His people. In addition, Leslie's 'Kingdom Keys' to the anointed will inspire and challenge you toward deeper intimacy with the Lord and enhanced awareness of the movements of the Spirit."

Ted Vail
Director, Foursquare Missions

"His passion for the supernatural, compassion for the suffering, and a life of intimacy with the Holy Spirit have taken him on a journey of some amazing experiences to confirm the 'Kingdom Keys' highlighted in this book."

Michael Dissanayeke
General Superintendent, Assemblies of God - Sri Lanka

"The Scriptures come alive through the lens of his real life stories that are certain to transform and forever impact the way you view the Word of God!"

Phil Liberatore
CPA, Marketplace Pastor & IRS Problem Solver

"Leslie Keegel lives what he teaches. He succinctly presents 'Kingdom Keys' that leave you freshly impacted by the power and beauty of the gospel. There is a fresh wind blowing, and Leslie has been swept by its power. Through the truths of this fascinating book, he invites us to participate. Come and dine!"

Wayne Cordeiro
New Hope Christian Fellowship – Hawaii

"This book is an exciting testament to the fact that Jesus Christ, through the Holy Spirit, will do the same, even greater, supernatural works in our day than He did during His earthly life. He just needs us to be available and willing to be His instruments in the same way as Dr. Keegel describes in this must-read book."

John Robb
Chairman, International Prayer Council
International Facilitator, World Prayer Assembly

"Based firmly on Scripture, its pages are also enriched with Dr. Keegel's inspiring experiences, having served through some of the most difficult years during the conflict situation in Sri Lanka. This book is a must-read for every Christian who desires to take his faith seriously and minister in the Spirit."

Deshamanya Godfrey Yogarajah
Deputy Secretary General, World Evangelical Alliance (WEA)
General Secretary, National Christian Evangelical Alliance of Sri Lanka
(NCEASL)

"Leslie's book is a must-read for people who are serious about figuring out how to walk in godly power and bringing the Kingdom of God to their world. I walked away from this book knowing that the Lord has more for me than the limited power that I have come to accept as inevitable."

Doug Graham
CEO and Co-founder, Continuant, Inc.

"I have no doubt whatsoever that this book will become an anointed book approved by the Lord that would make us all to fall on our knees seeking the Lord's forgiveness for all our wrongs committed during our ministries, seek our common God-given goal, and allow His anointing power to transform the lives of His called servants, individuals, communities, churches, and even nations."

Dhiloraj R.Canagasabey
Bishop of the Anglican Church, Colombo, Sri Lanka

"I believe that *The Spirit of the Lord is Upon Us* will put an end to powerless lives and ministries. The unusual miracles of Dr. Keegel's ministry combined with his ability to simply explain the mysteries surrounding God's intended life of power for the believer create much-needed confidence to act on God's word."

Jerry D. Dirmann
The Rock, Operation Solid Lives
Anaheim, CA

"My soul was uplifted and my heart for ministry renewed as I read of the Spirit's work in Sri Lanka. This book is a keeper."

Ralph Moore
Hope Chapel Founder

"Dr. Leslie Keegel has written a book that will both inspire you to do great things for God and challenge you to go to a new level of faith. He is a modern-day apostle who knows what it is to live out the book of Acts rather than just reading about it. You will be changed forever by reading *The Spirit of the Lord is Upon Us.*"

Cindy Jacobs
Generals International

"The simplicity and honesty of this book will catch you unaware, and before you realize what Dr. Keegel has done to minister to your spirit, you will find yourself filled with new levels of faith, and deeper understanding of the invisible realm."

Daniel A. Brown
International Bible Teacher and Author of *Embracing Grace*
and many other books

"I have watched, from the beginning of Leslie's ministry, a humble yet powerful servant of God impact tens of thousands of lives for Christ. His book is but a glimpse of that extraordinary journey, but it is an excellent one."

Paul Risser
Former President, The Foursquare Church

"The fruit of Leslie Keegel's remarkable ministry is very evident today. Here we have some of the stories that lie behind it. The noteworthy value of this book is that it demonstrates how scriptural truth is experienced in life and ministry. It will instruct God's servants and challenge them to launch out into powerful paths of Spirit-filled service."

Ajith Fernando
Teaching Director, Youth for Christ Sri Lanka
Author, *Jesus Driven Ministry*

"Leslie Keegel is a dynamic leader who has influenced my personal walk with Christ and ministry for over 20 years. *The Spirit of the Lord is Upon Us* explains how to tap into the gifts the Lord has given you and use them in dynamic ways. I am thankful for this book as it does not reach a single demographic, but can help the masses to stay on the course we are called to be on. Pastor Leslie Keegel has not only written a beautiful book, but he has lived his life as a godly example for all to witness."

Matthew Barnett
Co-Founder of The Dream Center
New York Times best selling author, *The Cause Within You*

ISBN: 978-0-692-92379-5

Library of Congress Control Number: 2017949652

Editor: Laurie De Revere
Cover Photo: Michael Kitada, michael@michaelkitada.com
Cover/Book Design: Wyce Ghiacy

Printed in the United States of America
1 2 3 4 5 20 19 18 17

Published and printed by Foursquare Missions Press
4905 E. La Palma Ave.
Anaheim, CA 92807

Visit www.foursquaremissionspress.org

FOREWORD BY DR. JACK HAYFORD

THE
SPIRIT
OF THE
LORD
IS UPON
US

DISCOVERING THE ANOINTING TO SHARE THE
GOSPEL, SET PEOPLE FREE, AND EXPERIENCE
THE SUPERNATURAL IN YOUR LIFE

DR. LESLIE KEEGEL
WITH ROBERT HUNT

DEDICATION

The Spirit of the Lord is Upon Us is dedicated to my beautiful
and patient wife, Belen. She has been the most encouraging
person in my life. She believes in me and stirs me up to keep
moving forward. Nothing much would have been accomplished
in me without the able assistance and blessings of Belen. We
together have seen many breakthroughs, faced scary moments
and overcome many a challenge of faith. My God-given, gifted
and anointed wife has stood by me through all situations and
seen me win every battle. I love you, my beloved friend and
companion. I am so grateful to Jesus for you.

TABLE OF CONTENTS

FOREWORD

I know of few spiritual leaders in today's Church who by every biblical standard would answer to the biblical description of a "first century church apostle." Leslie Keegel is such a person.

Nonetheless, without self-announced claims or any effort at parading his ministry or its fruits, he has for recent decades unto this moment evangelized a nation, and raised up thousands of leaders. By this means, from an original handful of people in a small congregation in Colombo he has raised up hundreds of churches and shaken this Asian nation unto the salvation of multitudes and by the great glory of God.

Those facts alone suffice to introduce a person…unless you want to let me add one more. Leslie Keegel is the most soft-spoken man I have ever met. His mannerisms bear the residual evidence of his background as an accountant. But at the same time, Leslie Keegel is as bold and faith-filled – animated by the love of God, with the sweet presence of the Holy Spirit in a ministry that consistently manifests in the miracles or multitudes coming to Christ and hundreds experiencing the healing power of the Savior – often with "signs following" miracles.

Leslie asked that I write the Foreword to this book. Frankly, it would make little difference to me what he wrote about, and I commend the context herein. He is one of the godliest men you will ever know, and I have ministered beside him on numerous occasions here in the USA, in Sri Lanka, and elsewhere.

Leslie is a proven, stable, trustworthy, Bible-centered lover of God, along with his wife, family, and all beside whom he serves.

May God be praised for all glory ultimately belongs to Him. However, Leslie would say the same thing – a hearty amen to that declaration.

Jack W. Hayford
Pastor Emeritus
The Church on the Way, Van Nuys, California
Founder and Chancellor
The King's University, Southlake, Texas

ACKNOWLEDGMENTS

Initially, I want to say a big thank you to Bob Hunt for his great contribution in writing this book. If not for his continuing encouragement and coaxing this would have never seen the light of day. You coached me, you asked me the right questions, and brought something out in me that I never felt I had. Each time I said I did not have what it takes to write a book, you argued and proved me wrong. Thank you Bob for all the effort, your time and expertise to see this book come out the beautiful way it has. I am very grateful to you for your selfless initiative. You have this amazing ability to bring out the best in people. May God bless you profusely.

I am also very grateful to the staff of Foursquare Missions Press for standing by me as we worked on the book. The ministry of the Foursquare Missions Press has been truly amazing. You have done wonderfully well by enhancing us in our evangelism and church planting efforts in Sri Lanka.

Secondly, I wish to thank my daughters, Blessie, Julie, Rosie and my son-in-law, Prince, for all the encouragement, advice and thoughts which they shared time to time. They have been a great help in the writing of this book from the beginning. Thank you for believing in me.

Thirdly, I wish to thank the Sri Lankan Foursquare Church, the General Supervisor, George Niranjan, the board members, the national office staff, the pastors and leaders of the Living Way Church, Dayantha, Dinesh, Romesh, Roger, Harim, and my assistant, Chinta, for all the prayers, support and encouragement they have given me. The stories in this book would not have been possible without your active partnership with me. My 36 years of service as national leader have been possible because you actively partnered with me selflessly.

Finally, I deeply appreciate the role Rev. Richard and Betty Kiser played in introducing me to the Foursquare fold in 1979. Dr. Don and Sally McGregor, the late Dr. Sam Middlebrook and Dr. John Amstutz were instrumental in discipling and mentoring me in the formative years of my ministry. Almost everything I know today is what they patiently taught me. I am very grateful to my great mentors.

THE
SPIRIT
OF THE
LORD
IS UPON
US

DISCOVERING THE ANOINTING TO SHARE THE
GOSPEL, SET PEOPLE FREE, AND EXPERIENCE
THE SUPERNATURAL IN YOUR LIFE

INTRODUCTION

My story comes mainly from my life and ministry in Sri Lanka, an island nation in South Asia near Southeast India. However, the move of God that I have experienced continues to reach far beyond the borders of my homeland, once called Ceylon.

This book was written to serve two purposes: One, to tell the story of the "Sri Lankan Miracle." Then to give insight and inspiration from both the Scripture and personal stories to move in the anointing of God. My hope is that the two will blend seamlessly together.

It is the power of the *gospel* (Greek – Evangelion), literally the "Good News," that sees lives transformed physically, spiritually, and emotionally. I am merely its student and it continues to instruct me daily.

The Bible modifies the single word *gospel* with a few descriptive phrases. For example: the Gospel of the Glory of Christ (2 Corinthians 4:4 NASB), the Gospel of Peace (Ephesians 6:15 NASB), and the Gospel of the Kingdom (Matthew 4:23, 9:35, 24:14 NASB). I have taken the liberty to use such descriptive phrases for the first seven chapter heads.

Chapter 1 The Gospel of Power

Chapter 2 The Gospel of Love and Compassion

Chapter 3 The Gospel of Reconciliation

Chapter 4 The Gospel of Re-Awakening

Chapter 5 The Gospel of Shalom

Chapter 6 The Gospel of Transformation

Chapter 7 The Gospel of His Return

Luke 4:18 encapsulates the mission of Jesus. His life on this earth was not limited to the spiritual, but extended, in a very real way, to the pain and suffering of humanity. And one cannot truly understand the personal life application of this verse without comprehending the self-limiting nature of the incarnation described in Philippians 2:6-8.

"Who, being in very nature God, did not consider equality with God something to be used to his own advantage; rather, he made himself nothing by taking the very nature of a servant, being made in human likeness. And being found in appearance as a man, he humbled himself by becoming obedient to death—even death on a cross!" (NIV)

Jesus depended on the anointing from his Father. He himself would plainly state that he only did that which he saw the Father doing. (John 5:19) Clearly, the mission of Jesus included a path for you and for me to walk, not only to know him, but also to know the power of his resurrection (and the fellowship of his suffering). (Philippians 3:10)

The vision I have both for the thousands of leaders in Sri Lanka and around the world that I have the privilege to serve alongside and for myself is this:

To rely completely on the anointing of the Holy Spirit to preach the message of the Good News to the poor, to minister healing and deliverance to the sick and bound, to set the discouraged and depressed free from hopelessness, and to speak the prophetic message of Jesus' return.

I have found in my numerous travels globally a lack of reliance upon this anointing by many in ministry. This is not to be critical – simply to make an observation, and most definitely not to communicate any sense of superiority…just the opposite. Apart from the anointing, you might be disappointed in me. Neither the most articulate nor charismatic, I can be extremely shy at times.

If the thousands who fill soccer stadiums or arenas to hear me preach met me beforehand, they might not want to stay after the worship. But if they remained, what they would hear and see would not be me in my weakness, but Him in his strength.

"'My grace is sufficient for you, for my power is made perfect in weakness.' Therefore I will boast all the more gladly about my weaknesses, so that Christ's power may rest on me."
2 Corinthians 12:9 (NIV)

I've read that if you are "not hungry for God, you're probably too full of yourself." Every believer faces the classic struggle of the flesh and spirit. The cup of our life cannot be filled with ourselves *and* Him. We will yield to one or the other.

A Global Vision

My vision for the Body of Christ, leader and lay person alike, based on the gospel and words spoken by Christ from Isaiah 61:

- To see all peoples reconciled to God through Jesus Christ
- To see all men and women who are reconciled to God be reconciled to one another irrespective of class, color, creed, nationality, and ethnicity or language
- To see the gospel of Jesus Christ impact seven spheres of influence – religion, family, governance, economy, education, health, and media
- To see all peoples become disciples of Christ who will become agents of change (salt and light) in their communities and market places
- To see prayer warriors and intercessors raised up globally who will pull down demonic strongholds and establish the Kingdom of God
- To see churches planted in every city and town around the world

This book will touch on all of the above as I have seen the gospel reach powerfully into each of these areas.

But there is so much more to do. The entreaties of our Lord are as true today as they were when he spoke them. They must be read with an even deeper sense of urgency because the time is short.

"…Behold, I say to you, lift up your eyes and look on the fields, that they are white for harvest." John 4:35b (NASB)

"The harvest is plentiful, but the laborers are few; therefore pray earnestly to the Lord of the harvest to send out laborers into his harvest." Matthew 9:37-38 (ESV)

I am praying for you – believing that if you haven't already joined those who work the fields, that you will do so. I'm believing for you to grow in the anointing of God, to become the sent laborer with a sharpened sickle.

I am praying for you, Pastor, whether your congregation lives in the streets of Colombo, Calcutta, or on the shores of California. Big, small, thriving, or surviving, I am believing that the words from this book will be used by the Holy Spirit to increase your thirst for the things of God.

And that nothing will quench that thirst except the very presence of God, the filling and anointing of the Holy Spirit.

<u>My Approach to Writing About the Anointing</u>

Over the years, I've been asked countless times to define "the anointing." I never quite feel satisfied with my answer. I suppose this book is written, in part, to best reply to the question.

However, I prefer description over definition. Maybe a small distinction, but one that satisfies my Eastern worldview bias toward narrative and story. For within the story, the Eastern mind would argue, one can more readily self-discover truth. An Eastern writer will rarely place the key truth (or thesis) in the beginning of a chapter, as we desire the reader to take more responsibility to glean understanding as the story unfolds. My apologies if this approach frustrates my Western friends.

My hope, ultimately, is that through the following pages, you, the reader, will be inspired by the stories to seek the anointing, not merely to intellectually grasp it. For the anointing does not lend itself easily to definition. Even a description of it falls woefully short. It is something to be experienced. And as you will read, it is not a light switch with an on and off button, but a lifestyle to be embraced. The late

John Wimber, in his seminal work *Power Evangelism,* stated it well:

"I do not believe it is enough for Christians to gather information and understand new facts – or even think differently about the supernatural in Scripture – if it does not affect how they live. At the core of my being, I am an activist."[1]

I pray we all become "activists" for the anointing of God.

Despite the above disclaimers, I briefly define and describe the anointing at the end of the book. Hopefully, it will simply summarize that which you have already ascertained. I will trust that you will resist the temptation to skip to the end.

Additionally, I've written prayers of impartation that are at the end of every chapter. How I wish to be able to meet and pray personally with all who read this book. It would give me great joy. Please know my prayers for you come from a special place in my heart.

1

The Gospel of Power

The wood ladder protested with every step up its weathered rungs until I reached the roof of an equally old house. My view was muted by the gray Bulgarian sky that hung like a wet canopy over the gathering people below. I began to pray.

Billed as the "Indian Preacher," which I thought a reference to my dark skin and South Asian features, the people were initially disappointed. They somehow expected an American Indian dressed in full native regalia, probably hoping for a bit of America's "Old West" experience, or at least the Hollywood version. I learned later that my skin color, similar to theirs, would suffice.

I began my sermon from this most unusual pulpit with a usual message – Jesus saves and Jesus heals. It was shorter than most, even with the translation. I finished by asking the crowd, now over a thousand, to respond to the gospel.

I always expect God to move in power. The Kingdom of God rarely takes territory from the Kingdom of Darkness in quiet. I may not always see the results at the altar, but I believe the same Jesus who felt compassion for the lost and sick always arrives on time.

It didn't take long for him to make an introduction to this community of Gypsies. I imagine this group, used to poverty and prejudice, reminded Jesus of his own people two thousand years ago.

And I got to watch it all from the rooftop.

One person, then two, then another lifted their bodies from makeshift wheelchairs, taking short steps that backed away the tightly packed crowd.

The cries that came from healing joined the whispers of astonishment. People screamed, people fell, hands were raised, and heads were bowed. It was as if Jesus walked through the crowd touching all he saw the Father touching.

I wanted to join the people, but my host demanded that I stay on the roof, fearing the crowd would crush me. My eye caught the sight of a young woman holding a baby. She held her infant with her healthy arm, but the other was deformed – it had stopped growing at the elbow with what looked like fingers protruding out.

I scanned across the horizon full of people being touched by the power of God, but was drawn back to the woman with the deformed arm. She had fallen under the weight of the glory of God. To this day, I don't know if she screamed in fear or if there was pain involved. But what happened next would nearly cause a panic in the crowd of people who watched.

Her deformed arm began to grow – I only wished I could have been closer to describe it more accurately. In a matter of minutes, God had restored to her a perfectly formed arm with perfectly functioning fingers.

Still, my Bulgarian host would not let me go down from the roof until all

> *It was as if Jesus walked through the crowd touching all he saw the Father touching.*

the people had gone. I watched, I wept, I prayed. When I finally descended the ladder, dozens of gypsy children, holding freshly picked wild flowers, came running toward me – their faces full of joy and wonder. I was the one who had brought the message and received their grateful gifts; but the truth was that I simply proclaimed the gospel and Jesus confirmed it in power.

The Church in Search of Power

"About three in the morning as we were continuing instant in prayer and the power of God came mightily upon us, insomuch that many cried out for exulting joy and many fell to the ground." — From the journal of John Wesley[1]

The pews of the Church universal are full of those who have never experienced the power of the gospel. Their personal lives lack transformation even as they recite the proper creeds and doctrines.

John Wesley encountered such a church in England some 300 years ago. Unfortunately, the powerless church knows no geographical or denominational boundaries. And time, despite the many glorious revivals, hasn't been the cure.

The Good News, or the gospel, is timeless. The impact that it had on the first century Jews or Gentiles is the same today for, in fact:

"Jesus Christ is the same yesterday, today, and forever."
Hebrews 13:8 (NKJV)

What has happened, however, is the steady separation of the proclamation of the gospel from the demonstration of the gospel. Both are the gospel. Words without power will never withstand the test of time. Power apart from the Word will lack context and meaning.

"…My message and my preaching were not in persuasive words of wisdom, but in demonstration of the Spirit and of power."
1 Corinthians 2:4 (NASB)

The church and its well-meaning leaders began to feel safe with the gospel's words, but not its power. Yes, the very word of God is transformational and powerful (two-edged sword), but in the hands of those who preach that its power is not for today, or those who preach it but do not demonstrate it, life is squeezed from its pages.

"The doctrine stating *signs and wonders are no longer needed because we have the Bible* was created by people who

hadn't seen God's power and needed an explanation to justify their own powerless churches." – Bill Johnson[2]

The fullness of the gospel is the heartbeat of the church. Its mission: To pulsate through the lives of the redeemed to the lost and hurting.

Pastor Jack and My Grandmother

I was a frustrated young minister in 1982. I knew the words of the Bible, but not the transformation that comes from them. One of my jobs was to copy tapes from the great Dr. Jack Hayford, who epitomized a minister who not only preached the gospel with intellectual fervor, but also demonstrated its power.

The messages from the tapes challenged my spirit. They opened my heart to its emptiness. I wanted more. I had seen signs as a young boy. My grandmother moved powerfully with the gift of the word of knowledge and the gift of healing. She would call me

"The fullness of the gospel is the heartbeat of the church. Its mission: To pulsate through the lives of the redeemed to the lost and hurting.

to her favorite chair and tell me things that the Lord showed her about me.

Sometimes they were words no nine year old wanted to hear. Something like, "Today, at one o'clock, you were at such and such place and did such and such bad thing."

She would pause to allow me to protest before I would repent. "Why, Grandma, do you always know these things about me and not my brothers?"

Her reply usually varied, but its essence was always, "Jesus loves you, Leslie, and has a great plan for your life."

Once I broke my arm. Before a doctor could be consulted, my grandmother intervened. She laid hands on the break and I winced in pain. Within moments, the pain was gone and the break was healed.

Yes, I knew about the Gospel of Power, but I wouldn't learn until later that the richest gift from the Lord is the intimacy he offers to all. And I caught a glimpse of it when my two-year-old daughter climbed into my arms.

A Heartbeat Away

I had just finished copying Dr. Hayford's latest sermon for pastors in the Philippines. The Philippines will always hold a special place in my heart. It is where I met my beautiful wife, Belen, and where I studied at Bible college.

My daughter, Blessie, a lively and loquacious two-year-old, followed me into my study room. It was four in the morning; she was awake and I was consumed by a lack of intimacy with God. She jumped into my lap and held me close. Pressing her cheek on my chest she said, "What's that?" startled by the rhythmic beat.

"That's my heart."

Her obvious question from the mind of a two-year-old followed. "Do I have one?"

"Yes you do," I said, pointing to her tiny chest.

Contented, she fell asleep in my arms, as secure as any very loved child could be.

In the quiet and stillness of that moment, the Lord began to speak to me. "My son, I want you to live in a place where you fall into my arms, close to hear my heart. Leslie, I want your heart to beat to the rhythm of my heart."

I will never forget that moment. I draw upon it to this day. It is the foundation of my life and the cornerstone of my ministry.

"Are you tired? Worn out? Burned out on religion? Come to me. Get away with me and you'll recover your life. I'll show you how to take a real rest. Walk with me and work with me—watch how I do it. Learn the unforced rhythms of grace. I won't lay anything heavy or ill-fitting on you. Keep company with me and you'll learn to live freely and lightly." Matthew 11:28-30 (The Message)

Power comes from intimacy. Intimacy exists only in complete trust. And trust is birthed from grace.

That grace can be lived out daily. It can flow, even unnoticed, until it's interrupted by our sin. Like the beating of the heart, its rhythm quiets our spirit because it rests in His Spirit.

It is in that place of unforced rhythms of grace that we can *"be still and know that I am God." (Psalm 46:10)*

This is the beginning and ending place for the anointing. We live in a world enamored by short cuts. We prefer social media over real relationship. Living with others is hard work, so we slip into a form of isolation pretending we're social because we're on Facebook, Twitter, or Instagram.

> *Power comes from intimacy. Intimacy exists only in complete trust. And trust is birthed from grace.*

We are even more willing to escape relationship when the object is God. Our relationship with him can develop into the classic unhealthy "approach/avoidance."[3] But he demands more and will not compromise. He is jealous for our time and will not share it with another.

Take a Bold Step

Those in the Western world love "keys" or "steps."

This first Kingdom Key began for me with my two-year-old sleeping soundly on my chest years ago.

Kingdom Key #1

The level of anointing that will flow from you is based on the level of relationship that has filled you. You want to impart God's heart to others? How much of his heart fills yours?

Search me, O God, and know my heart: try me,
and know my thoughts.
Psalm 139:23 (KJV)

Do you want the power of God to flow from you? Have you opened up your life to the Holy Spirit to search your heart – even to the deepest, darkest corners?

Do you want to give wise counsel? Have you spent enough time with the Master to say with the Apostle Paul, "Let this mind be in you, which was also in Christ Jesus"[4]?

You can't give away something you do not possess.

I spend everyday in God's presence – some days more time, some less, but everyday in an ongoing dialogue with my Creator. Everyday I, like the children initially stopped by the disciples, climb on Jesus' lap to listen to his heart, and to find my rest.

> **"You can't give away something you do not possess.**

To not do so would be spiritual and ministerial malpractice. I understand it might be easier for those much more gifted than I to skip this time, but I cannot.

In Sri Lanka, as in many nations, you cannot walk out the door without expecting to encounter a need or challenge that cries out for the anointing of God. And sometimes, you don't even need to leave the house.

Demonic encounters along with severe persecution have naturally helped the Sri Lankan church to grow strong and mature. The gospel message we preach by necessity must be given both by proclamation and in power.

In my nation, Christianity is a minority. We are followed in size by Islam, Hinduism, and Buddhism. Though it is a place of great beauty, it is also a land of great darkness. John Wimber's phrase "Power Encounter"[5] is an everyday occurrence. I have been the object of hundreds of such encounters, often with local witch doctors attempting to place curses on me. Some in the West would dismiss any idea of curses as being hysterical nonsense, but I would advise against being too flippant when being challenged by the agents of demonic forces.

If you doubt me, please visit Sri Lanka and maybe you can experience something like what occurred in my office a few years ago.

The Serpent King

One of my pastors noticed a man showing off at a bus station in town. He performed what could best be described as acrobatic feats on a bicycle, obviously aided by outside forces – all the while proclaiming, "I am the most powerful man in Sri Lanka. No one is more powerful!" The repetition of this claim irritated the pastor to the point of issuing a rather ill advised challenge: "Not true. My pastor (me) is more powerful than you." As if the challenge wasn't enough, he proceeded to give the man my name and address.

Normally my assistant sets appointments and controls the flow of traffic into my office. She never allows someone from the street to walk into my office without first letting me know.

To this day, she says she never saw him enter.

The first thing I noticed was his eyes. The old saying "eyes are the window to the soul" is often true, but better the words of Jesus:

"The lamp of the body is the eye. If therefore your eye is good, your whole body will be full of light. But if your eye is bad, your whole body will be full of darkness. If therefore the light that is in you is darkness, how great is that darkness!" Matthew 6:22-23 (NKJV)

His eyes were wild and they were full of darkness. He stood a few feet away, probably in his 40s, fairly large especially for a Sri Lankan, no beard or crazy hair. You'd probably pass him by unnoticed unless he spoke to you, then you would notice. His voice was powerful and his demeanor when he spoke intimidating.

"I'm here," he proclaimed as if I had been waiting for him. My reply wasn't calculating but it took immediate control. "Now that you are here, sit down."

He got to the point quickly, "If you want to know who I am . . ." He paused briefly. "I am the god of the Serpent Kingdom."

Once again, my friends living in the West might too quickly dismiss such a character as a madman. In fact, I initially had the same reaction. But, in Sri Lanka, demonic forces are more open to express themselves through willing participants.

He was willing and gave quite a startling statement, "Say your goodbyes for it will be your last breath." He was, if anything, dramatic. I didn't, however, doubt his next statement,

"I have millions of demons and am going to release them one by one."

"Say your goodbyes for it will be your last breath.

What you're about to read may cause you to question either my sanity or my integrity. I hope you can trust that both are operating under the Lordship of Jesus Christ.

Emanating from his body came some of the most hideous, translucent faces, both human and animal-like. Some were faces that fit neither category, but were ugly all the same. All came from hell.

As each one thrust toward me, I rebuked them in the name of Jesus. For some reason, I was led to not speak to these entities, but to alternate between kicking them or slapping them as they came into my personal space.

As I did so, they simply dissolved and neither touched nor entered me. He may have been exaggerating about "millions," but not by much as this went on for an hour and a half.

The man, exasperated and extremely angry at the demons failure to harm me, finally fell on his face. He looked up at me and said, "You are the greatest. Let me out of here. I want to go!"

I felt compassion for him and wanted freedom for this man, obviously imprisoned in years of darkness.

"Do you really want to go without opening your heart to Jesus?"

The power of the gospel is the divine truth that the Creator of all so loved the world, his creation, that he made the ultimate sacrifice, sending his only son to die for our sins and resurrect so we might live in his light.

"You are the light of the world." Matthew 5:14a (NKJV)

Light will always expel the darkness. We must be a reflection of his light. We can illuminate his light if we allow enough in, to expose all things hiding in the dark.

The man understood and received the Good News. He wanted to tell the world about me, "Why can't you take advantage of yourself? I'm going to tell everyone!" he exclaimed in an innocent manner. But God's glory must never be shared. I told him not to tell others. It was an important first lesson for a new believer to know. He began attending one of our churches.

Kingdom Key #2

Anointing of the Holy Spirit is given to people to demonstrate God's love and power in accordance with the Bible, not for any self-glory. But you must be willing to step out in it at any time.

Preach the word; be prepared in season and out of season; correct, rebuke and encourage – with great patience and careful instruction.
2 Timothy 4:2 (NIV)

VIP

The power of the gospel is not always so confrontational. Sometimes it comes in the form of a tasteful amount of salt meant to flavor, not overwhelm. It draws people to *"taste and see that the Lord is good." Psalm 34:8 (NKJV)*

"You are the salt of the earth." Matthew 5:13a (NIV)

It's not always the blinding glare of a searchlight looking into our souls. The anointing that flows can be a warm and joyful thing. By the way, if your personality is so "prophetic" that it lacks joy and warmth, you need more time in his presence.

Once, I was invited by the president of a nation to their office. I must withhold the name of this country, as it could become a problem in this nation not fond of Christianity.

The president's assistant told me I would have only 15 minutes. Our meeting, which ended up lasting an hour, was pleasant enough. However, it was the last few minutes that I fondly recall.

"Can you explain to me why the very moment you walked in and sat down, the atmosphere changed? Please explain it."

Not a bad opening to share the gospel.

"It's the presence of the Lord Jesus who lives in us. He goes with us where we go. And where he is welcomed, he brings peace and joy."

> *"By the way, if your personality is so "prophetic" that it lacks joy and warmth, you need more time in his presence.*

After a few more exchanges, the president was grateful and expressed happiness that I had come. He then asked me what they could do for me. It was clear that just about any favor could be mine.

Power like that can be tempting. The Tempter himself tried unsuccessfully to use it on Jesus at the end of 40 days of fasting. Jesus' answer was to quote the Scripture. One of the many reasons every believer must fill their mind with the Word of God – if Jesus used it as a tool against evil, why shouldn't we?

I made sure the president's eyes were focused on mine and clarified that God had sent me only to bless, not request.

"Strange, most people want something. You want to bless me. I've never experienced that before."

Kingdom Key #3

The anointing comes as we abide in his presence. It will bring forth fruit like peace and joy into any situation giving God all the glory.

If you abide in Me, and My words abide in you,
you will ask what you desire, and it shall be done
for you. By this My Father is glorified, that you
bear much fruit; so you will be My disciples.
John 15:7-8 (NKJV)

The famous and disputed statement of St. Francis is often misunderstood and misapplied, "Preach the gospel at all times and use words if necessary."[6] His words (or whoever originated them) only make sense if one is living in such a way that they are so full of the Spirit that it actually can invade the atmosphere of a room.

I've experienced, too many times to count, walking into a situation and encountering an atmosphere, a literal, even physical presence, that was changed by the presence of God in me.

"…greater is He who is in you than he who is in the world."
1 John 4:4b (NASB)

Do we believe this? If so, we should also believe that we can impact for the Kingdom anywhere we go or whoever we encounter.

"For our gospel did not come to you in word only, but also in power and in the Holy Spirit and with full conviction . . ."
1 Thessalonians 1:5a (NASB)

Elvis, The Beatles, and a Promise

As a fairly rebellious teenager, I loved Elvis and the Beatles. Yes, I know that's hard to imagine for those who know me now. I would sneak out at night and join the youth of the Pentecostal Church who in the day lived under legalism, but at night prayed for hours until taking a break to listen to Rock and Roll.

These same kids invited me to a meeting where a "cool preacher is coming." That man was a preacher from New Zealand.

I was swayed to attend with the promise, "After the meeting we will listen to the Beatles."

It didn't take long for the preacher to make me feel uncomfortable, pointing his finger at me and yelling. "You! God has a plan for your life!"

I looked behind me, hoping he was referring to someone else, but he came running up to me. My little Sri Lankan body was petrified.

"I'm talking to you. Tomorrow, you and I will have a meeting."

> "*Just get me out of here. Give me John, Paul, George, and Ringo!*

I just stared ahead – speechless. No way I was going to meet him. Just get me out of here. Give me John, Paul, George, and Ringo!

Falling into the Future

Something inside me (of course the Holy Spirit) pushed me to meet with this preacher. I couldn't believe I was going. He didn't waste any time laying his hands on my head and saying a quick prayer.

Before I knew it, I was lying on the floor under what I would learn was the power of God. This was not how I planned to spend my afternoon, but the experience of warm waves of love filling my mind and body was pretty "cool" for an 18-year-old. It seemed I had left this world.

When I returned to a state of full consciousness, I saw the preacher sitting there laughing at me, eating a mango and drinking tea.

Then his prophecy over me changed the course of my life. It filled me with a purpose and was the seed planted for a big vision I would later receive.

"He will empower you. He will use you to take his gospel around the world."

He then instructed me to assist him at his meetings. I would see the most powerful moves of God I have ever experienced. Not a bad mentorship for an 18-year-old. The gospel was preached, and the gospel was demonstrated. I would never be the same.

Kingdom Key #4

To grow in the anointing of God, find someone who clearly moves in it and spend as much time as possible to learn all you can.

When they had crossed, Elijah said to Elisha, "Tell
me, what can I do for you before
I am taken from you?"
"Let me inherit a double portion of your spirit,"
Elisha replied.
2 Kings 2:9 (NIV)

*D*ear *Lord, when you walked on the earth you*
functioned under the powerful anointing of the Holy
Spirit. As a result of you functioning in the fullness of the
Spirit you did great wonders, healed the sick, and set people
free from demons. Dear Lord, it is my prayer that you would
fill us with your Spirit to function in great power. My prayer
for you at this moment is that the Lord will release His
power upon you in a mighty way to experience miracles and
the ability to heal the sick. In Jesus' name I pray.

2

THE GOSPEL OF LOVE AND COMPASSION

I know the feeling. I've experienced it, unfortunately, too many times before. Yet this time was unusually powerful.

As our plane neared the tarmac of the Los Angeles International Airport, better known as LAX, I began my usual habit of speaking in tongues. I pray both in the Spirit and with my mind, asking the Lord for wisdom and His words. This was an especially important missions conference since I had been invited to speak by my hero in the faith, Dr. Jack Hayford.

After disembarking, I made my way to Immigration – it's there where I felt a particularly strong demonic presence.

Ushered into a cubicle just outside the main immigration lines, I was instructed to wait for another officer. She entered the room, barely looking at me, and immediately began the interview, which resembled more of an interrogation. Whatever questions she asked of me, she responded to my answer with an angry, "You're not telling the truth!" I had never encountered such hostility in all my travels.

Finally she proclaimed, "I have the power to send you out of this country in 24 hours."

Exasperated, I responded kindly but forcefully, "I don't know what to tell you…I've been telling you the truth."

She proceeded to toss the clothes from my suitcase onto the floor until she came across my Bible, which she promptly tossed across the table at me.

Her next question was unexpected. "You mean to tell me you read this?"

My answer took her off guard. "I not only read it, I believe it and preach it with all of my heart."

Her demeanor began to change as she pointed at the Bible and looked at me with an almost childlike earnestness. "After you read it, believe it, and preach it, what happens?"

"All kinds of miracles happen." I proceeded to share a few that came to mind. "If you want me to verify it, I can do that." She seemed to finally believe what I shared by way of testimonies.

My heart changed. Contempt had turned to compassion. Immediately, the presence of God filled this tiny room and an anointing came over me, prompting me to speak to her tenderly but boldly.

"I have a message the Lord has shown me about you – three different things." I hesitated for an instant to see if she wanted me to continue. "You hate your parents. In fact, you left home today with the intention of never going back."

Her head was down, staring at the floor, but listening intently. It got even more personal.

"You have a hormonal disease."

Hearing that, she immediately looked up at me and asked, "How did you know that?"

"It is the Holy Spirit." With those words, she began to weep. I asked her if I could pray for her.

Laying my hands on the top of her head, she began to fall under the power of the Holy Spirit. One can imagine explaining to another immigration officer why their fellow agent was lying on the floor. So I took my hand off her, but continued to pray.

I never have been so grateful for a hug and a stamped passport ever before or since.

"Please let me know, Leslie, if there's ever anything you need."

Kingdom Key #5

The gospel comes in power, but also in love and compassion. God's anointing is never demonstrated without love.

And though I have the gift of prophecy, and understand all mysteries and all knowledge, and though I have all faith, so that I could remove mountains, but have not love, I am nothing.
1 Corinthians 13:2 (NKJV)

Mission of Love

I love Sri Lanka. I love all its people with the tenderness that comes from God. There are many in this nation who have suffered so much from the 25 years of civil war, and the atrocities that come with war. Every family in some way was affected.

> *"The gospel comes in power, but also in love and compassion. God's anointing is never demonstrated without love.*

Add to this the pervasive spiritual oppression, and the intolerance of other religions, and you have a nation, like an open wound, desperately in need of healing that only Christ's love can bring.

In that context, the decision to preach and demonstrate the gospel of love and compassion came naturally. We proceeded to send dozens, hundreds of teams, into the nation, trained and prayed up with the mission to love the people.

No preaching until they are loved and cared for. If the mission from the Lord wasn't so clear to me, I would have doubted our strategy. But soon, the results came in.

It was normal to hear testimonies begin with expressions of amazement from people of other faiths. "You're different (referring to one of our workers). You don't beat your wife, how come?" And then the opportunity to proclaim the truth came.

Still, the gospel of power needed to always be evident. Before entering any area, we always would do what we called "spiritual mapping"[1] and find where the local principalities and powers resided. We prayed and cast down those forces, tilling the fallow ground, making ready for harvest.

Priests in villages would openly declare Christians can and should be killed. Death threats were, and are even now, common. Yet, love always wins. But love is hard, especially when all you have loved has been taken by hate.

Unspeakable Tragedy

During the civil war, worshipers in one of our house churches gathered after returning from a successful youth camp. Spirits were high and the worship heartfelt.

At the same time, soldiers seeking revenge from an earlier bomb explosion burst into this meeting. There is no record of what was said, only what was done. All 16 worshipers were shot and the house set on fire. What they found in the aftermath stunned even the most hardened cynic.

Charred bodies found with hands clasped together surrounding a Bible, opened and not burned.

The head of the home, a Hindu, was the only member of the family who survived the attack, as he was away at work in the field. He came to Colombo to attend the memorial service where I preached. Despite his loss and his incalculable pain, he listened to the gospel of love and compassion.

Only the Holy Spirit could reach into such a grieving heart and bring healing. He received Christ and remains faithful, never bitter, to this day.

I've been personally threatened many times. There was a $10,000 price for my death for nearly a year. Once, my neighbor was killed because the killers, not knowing I shared the same address with my neighbor, went to house "A." We lived in "B."[2]

I learned of this "mistake" when I overheard a conversation between two people who didn't know who I was. Needless to say, we moved...quickly.

> *But the answer is never revenge, only more love.*

But the answer is never revenge, only more love. And this is not some

45

temporal love or affection, but love rooted in "For God so loved the world that He gave…"

Kingdom Key #6

The anointing to share the Gospel of Love must come from being loved. In all our sin, all our failings, he still loves us. Can we do any less to those he loves?

But God demonstrates his own love for us in this:
While we were still sinners, Christ died for us.
Romans 5:8 (NIV)

Former Catholic priest, Brennan Manning, insightfully states, **"God loves you unconditionally, as you are and not as you should be, because nobody is as they should be."**[3]

The Blind Shall See and Deaf Hear

"Impossible odds set the stage for amazing miracles."

— Mark Batterson[4]

Planting house churches is my passion and vision. Yes, of course, large, beautiful buildings are a blessing, yet they are impractical and often dangerous when placed in areas hostile to the gospel. The buildings can inadvertently become symbols of religious aggression to the local people. Our mission is always to come in love and compassion.

So, as I sat in the back of the car being driven to a new house church meeting in an area of Sri Lanka known to be closed to the gospel, I was particularly grateful. And I love being around young, faithful pastors who are full of passion, willing to lay down their lives for the gospel.

The two in the front seat of the car were men of such character. They shared about their vision, plans, and challenges in starting churches in unfriendly villages and towns.

One of them began to tell me of a local school run by leaders of another religion. The 22 children of this small school were all either blind or deaf. What they said next shocked me, and frankly, upset me. "Well, Pastor, we told them you are coming . . ." That part didn't really get my attention; the second part did. "…and when you come, all the children will be healed."

Now, I have prayed and seen blind eyes open and the deaf recover their hearing. I've also seen the dead come back to life (more on that later). But, moving in the anointing of God means to follow the pattern of Jesus who said, *"I only do that which I see the Father do." (John 5:19)* I never like to presume the Lord's moving.

I wanted them to turn the car around. Yet, these wonderful young pastors, I couldn't let them down. I began to pray.

We entered the building of these children who had gathered for our arrival. The head priest was away, but the administrator greeted us warmly. Some of the parents were there as well.

I told the gathering, "You must have faith in Jesus," then proceeded to tell them in simple, clear language who he was and is. I led them all in a sinner's prayer.

I spoke directly to the children, all under 10 years of age – beautiful children of God who were eager to listen.

"Something good is going to happen to you." You could see the excitement in their faces. "Some of you cannot see, but will be able to see. Some of you cannot hear, but will be able to hear." I paused as a person delivered my words in sign language. Laying hands on each of their precious heads, I prayed, full of faith and belief.

Have you ever seen the face of a child at Christmas?

Their healing came quickly. We immediately tested each of them; all were completely healed.

The priest returned the following day. He was not happy.

"Moved with compassion, Jesus touched their eyes; and immediately they regained their sight and followed Him."
Matthew 20:34 (NASB)

Want to move in the anointing of God? Be willing to step out in faith even when you want to "turn around" and leave a seemingly impossible situation. Peter must have felt the chill of doubt course through his body before his walk on water. Faith will come as you need it, and know that the Gospel of Power loves to join the Gospel of Compassion.

The heart of God is mercy and he depends upon us to display his heart. The same Jesus who was "moved with compassion" two thousand years ago to see blind

> *The heart of God is mercy and he depends upon us to display his heart.*

people see is still moved with equal compassion. Why not the same results?

Kingdom Key #7

The person moving under the anointing of God will be a conduit of his compassion.

That I may know Him and the power of His resurrection, and the fellowship of His sufferings, being conformed to His death.
Philippians 3:10 (NKJV)

Compassion for the Tormented

Moving in the anointing of God is like most things, a process of learning. No one wakes up one day before ever casting out even one demon and decides to start a deliverance ministry. You watch. You learn. You do.

In Sri Lanka, the learning curve can get shortened quickly because the need is so confrontational. I wish my Western friends could see more of the power of the gospel to confront the enemy – I believe it would hasten revival.

Newly filled in the Spirit and full of "Go ye," I went with a group of young friends village to village to pass out hand bills for an evangelistic conference. As we came upon one house, a young girl, possibly 16, greeted us in her yard. The greeting caught me by surprise. She took off one of her slippers and slapped me across the face. She proceeded to move to larger more lethal objects, taking a chair as her next weapon.

Where were my friends? Right behind me, of course, cowering in fear. The girl wasn't merely agitated, she was obviously possessed.

I had watched the pastor who mentored me cast out many demons in the short time under his mentorship. My grandmother also took authority over principalities. Now it was my turn.

"I rebuke you in Jesus name!" She immediately fell flat, backwards. Her mother came running up to us, seeing her daughter writhing on the ground. Instead of anger, she was apologetic. "I am so sorry, my daughter is demon possessed." She began to tell us a sad tale of taking her afflicted daughter to many priests and then to a witch doctor, all with negative results.

Her words stirred a great compassion in our hearts.

"No one in the world can help her. Thank you for being so kind, you are fine young fellows." She went on, exasperated and hopeless. "The demons will kill her. I expect this." The demons, speaking through the voice of the girl, would often proclaim this lie to her mother.

My friends and I were filled in equal parts angry at the devil and sympathy for the mother and daughter.

The Exorcism

Collectively, we had little experience casting out demons. So our first course of action was to take this shy 16-year-old, who moved in and out of demonic manifestations, to the deliverance meeting.

However, it quickly became clear that this was a case of *"this kind does not go out except by prayer and fasting."* *Matthew 17:21 (NKJV)* So much for an easy prayer.

So you want the anointing of God? You want to move in his power and see people set free? Sometimes before seeing the power of his resurrection, you must live in the fellowship of his sufferings. (Philippians 3)

We prayed for the girl for four days straight – no sleeping, no eating.

Yes, quite probably, the extended time we took was based on our inexperience and lack of authority. But whether you're casting out multiple demons or consoling someone dying of cancer, you must be committed to the process. No shortcuts. No lazy response.

Each day, two demons left her. Their first line of attack: scare us. "We're going to kill all of you!" she screamed in an ugly, otherworldly voice.

They then turned to mocking, even to the point of making my friends laugh at me – all to distract, to keep us from praying.

Kingdom Key #8

The enemy will use your vulnerabilities to distract you from your purpose. Even Jesus faced temptation that would have taken him from his ultimate purpose, the cross.

Again, the devil took him to a very high mountain and showed him all the kingdoms of the world and their splendor.
Matthew 4:8 (NIV)

After four days, the final demons left her, except one – the most powerful one.

"Now you are confronting me, but you cannot cast me out!"

Never listen to the enemy's lies.

Once he was expelled, her face transformed. Her unnatural strength left her and she eagerly both accepted Christ and was immersed in the Holy Spirit. Even her mother got saved and filled in the Spirit. Others came to Christ when they saw the power of the gospel.

I learned so much during those four days. Moving in authority, in the anointing, is a learning process and it can come at a cost. But the most important lesson was found in experiencing God's great compassion for the downtrodden, the afflicted, the hurting.

Do you see where the enemy is killing, destroying, and stealing? Know the charge of Jesus is, *"I came that they may have life, and have it abundantly."* John 10:10 (NASB)

He is seeking believers who will be his hands and know his heart. All he asks is for you to make the first step, then trust him to lead the rest of the way.

> *Moving in authority, in the anointing, is a learning process and it can come at a cost.*

*D*ear Lord, we read in Matthew 9:36 that as you saw the crowds of people you saw them weary and scattered like sheep having no shepherd. You were moved with compassion at that sight.

You had mercy on people, pitied them, and ministered to them with great compassion. Your compassion poured like a river and it is your loving compassion that healed the sick, raised the dead, cast out demons, and fed the 5,000 and 4,000. Dear Lord, grant us your compassion. I pray that the Lord will fill your heart with great compassion. Dear Lord, I release your compassion to minister to people with heart-felt divine compassion. In Jesus' name, amen.

3

THE GOSPEL OF RECONCILIATION

"All this is from God, who reconciled us to himself through Christ

and gave us the ministry of reconciliation: that God was reconciling

the world to himself in Christ, not counting people's sins against

them. And he has committed to us the message of reconciliation."

2 Corinthians 5:18-19 (NIV)

I was walking down a dirt road, Bible in hand, excited to share my testimony with a small gathering in a neighboring village — until I saw a man only a few yards ahead: my father.

We greeted each other, barely. No hug or handshake, no asking where the other was heading.

The Beatles wrote a song, "The Long and Winding Road." Our walk was just that, winding and very silent, and it got more uncomfortably long with each step.

And it would get worse.

I grew up fearing my father. Fear turned to hate. His weapons were words and fists. "You're useless," hurt almost as much as a closed hand to the face – almost.

But nothing hurt worse than when he beat my dear mother. The rage it created in my heart caused me to dream of his murder. However, killing him would only make my mother's life even more unbearable.

Words are powerful. I've felt their deep, penetrating thrust into my heart, but those two words built my first self-image, "You're useless."

I meditated on them. I believed them. I acted out based on them. One teacher predicted my future...in prison.

Anger took root to fill the big, empty void. It would take the Holy Spirit to replace anger, hurt, and betrayal with love.

> *It would take the Holy Spirit to replace anger, hurt, and betrayal with love.*

"For if while we were enemies we were reconciled to God through the death of His Son, much more, having been reconciled, we shall be saved by His life." Romans 5:10 (NASB)

My father and I walked until we came upon our destination. "Where are you going?" I finally asked.

"A prayer meeting."

Shocked barely described my reaction. "A lady invited me," he continued.

"Your first time?" I asked, searching for anything to say.

"Yes." He asked me, "Where are you going?"

"The prayer meeting."

I should have been thrilled – my father, someone desperately in need of God, going to a prayer meeting. Instead, I looked for a way out. I couldn't find any.

He sat right in front of me as I was placed in the speaker's spot in the room. We sang, but I could barely mouth the words as worship failed to compete with all the memories and emotions.

My father had no idea I was the guest speaker. And I had no idea how to share my testimony, a life story of anger, hate, violence, and thoughts of suicide, all based on two words he spoke often to me.

"You're useless," the enemy enjoyed reminding me as the worship continued. I couldn't look at my father.

Words can curse, but words can bless.

I used words, from both the Scripture and from my heart to share my life and the gospel – the power of the gospel to change a life.

That day, my father gave his life to God. He never got violent or angry again. He reconciled with my mother, reconciled with his family, reconciled with himself.

Family First

When someone thinks about the power of the gospel and the anointing of God, it's easy to focus on a miraculous healing or a deeply revealing and accurate word of knowledge. However, nothing compares to a life changed, a human life that once stumbled in darkness, now dancing in the light.

"And although you were formerly alienated and hostile in mind, engaged in evil deeds, yet He has now reconciled you in His fleshly body through death, in order to present you before Him holy and blameless and beyond reproach." Colossians 1:21-22 (NASB)

Man reconciled to God, and therefore man reconciled to man. What can demonstrate God's power more than that?

Kingdom Key #9

If your preaching is anointed, it will always result in lives reconciled to God and man.

But God demonstrates His own love toward us, in that while we were yet sinners, Christ died for us.
Romans 5:8 (NASB)

Like the old expression, "charity begins at home," reconciliation must begin there too. If the gospel is truly about reconciliation, it can and should impact our own families. And like our walk with Christ that moves from "glory to glory," reconciliation is often a layer-by-layer process. As in all aspects in our spiritual walk, it must grow and that takes time, like the relationship with my father. Though my father believed in Christ, went to church, and faithfully read his Bible, our relationship could not be described as tender.

It would often take my wife's, Belen's, loving touch to bridge the gap between a father and son who were struggling to learn about each other. Her unbridled enthusiasm for life could sweep over any hint of our apathy or awkward silence. Belen could make the Mona Lisa burst out into laughter.

Her gift and willingness to use it with my father edged us, however grudgingly, closer together. She saw the need: a stubborn father and son who desperately wanted to love each other, but lacked the history and skill set to do so.

She was the instrument of reconciliation between a father and son. Every one of us is called at some time in our life to be that instrument to another. To miss that opportunity is to miss God.

She didn't preach, she didn't shame; she lavishly loved. Love has this wonderful way of spilling over into nearby lives. Love of life is infectious; it spreads even to hearts hardened by years of neglect. The French even have a phrase for it: "la joie de vivre" – the joy of living.

> *Love of life is infectious; it spreads even to hearts hardened by years of neglect.*

Belen has *la joie de vivre* in buckets, but it was her willingness to use it that set the table for one of the most powerful personal moments in my life – a moment that would begin to show me God's bigger picture for the Church's role in bringing reconciliation to the world.

The Day Before

Have you ever been asked an unexpected question from an unexpected person? When my father asked me one Saturday afternoon, "What's your vision, Leslie?" his words nearly short-circuited my brain. I recovered quickly, however, and pulled out a map of Sri Lanka and began to share my vision to shepherd an entire nation.

In the past, I would have been met with silence or a grudging acknowledgment, but this time proved different. He looked me in the eye, something he'd rarely done, and said, "I am deeply impressed." I thought he liked my plans, but his words quickly changed to the very personal.

"Son, I've watched your life. It has deeply touched me. I've watched how you grew as a young person, your priorities, and it changed me."

There is nothing a son craves more from his father than to hear words of admiration and respect.

"Son, I'd like to call you my pastor."

The next day would be my father's last on this earth.

Let Your Family be a Testimony

We opened our umbrellas to keep us dry from the monsoon rain. We watched as the rats crisscrossed each other looking for dry ground. We did this while sitting on mats inside the tiny cardboard home with the coconut palm thatched roof.

Nothing unusual about it – a fairly typical evening Bible study in the slums of Colombo.

To some of our Western friends, exposing our children to such an experience is nearly unforgivable. After all, are not our children to be the center of our lives, to be protected at all cost? Of course we prayed, pleading the blood, after every visit. We knew that our children regularly came across sick and diseased children and adults. And illness posed the least of the dangers living among the poorest of the poor. We thank the Lord our daughters never experienced any diseases.

Nothing speaks louder to someone hearing about being reconciled to God than seeing you trusting God with your own family. God, the Father, entrusted his only Son into the hands of a young Jewish couple. 30 years later, Jesus didn't just appear one day on the stage; he had lived among the people he would preach to.

The people living in the cardboard shacks of Colombo knew the Keegels, all five of us. Our message of the gospel, often accompanied by signs and wonders, rang true to those who witnessed it. The truth came from a willingness to experience all the fears, the shame, the lack that our neighbors knew. And when the joy, the love, the peace broke through, it was birthed in a soil deep and rich in trust. Of course, it is always good for your neighbors to see the power of God in your everyday life.

Kingdom Key #10

Do those that see you live life trust the words you speak? The anointing is not reserved for a church platform only; it grows in the laboratory called Life. The anointing is the empowerment to live the way Christ desires us to live.

He who says he abides in Him ought himself also to
walk just as He walked.
1 John 2:6 (NKJV)

Julie

"Julie, come pray for me. I'm dying!"

I added the last part for personal effect, knowing full well my two-year-old daughter had yet to grasp the meaning of mortality.

Scheduled to speak in a series of outreaches in the eastern part of Sri Lanka, I fell ill. Lying on a well-worn couch, trying to sleep in between episodes of various forms of sickness, Julie blissfully unaware came into the room, running and spinning.

She was quick to heed my entreating. After all, she and her two sisters were "experienced" faith healers. Often after service, they would line up the other children and play church. This involved, among other liturgical duties, the casting out of demons and the laying on of hands for the sick. Who says children get bored in "Big Church"? They absorb much more than we know.

So, Julie knew the routine and laid her hands on my stomach. *How sensitive to the Spirit,* I thought, she knew where the virus lay in wait. Her prayer, however, caught me by surprise.

"Jesus," a good start, to the point, taking authority in the most powerful name in the universe. "Jesus, bless this food!"

After the declarative prayer, she went about her business, supremely confident in the power of God.

Strangely, I fell asleep immediately. I woke up perfectly healthy, even able to attend the meeting, which resulted in a new church planting.

Children can walk in a natural, powerful anointing with God. We must study them, as Jesus suggested, to measure how far we've fallen as adults from the purity and innocence of their trust.

I wonder if we are not cheating both them and ourselves when we expect little in regard to their capacity to minister. What if churches

> *Children can walk in a natural, powerful anointing with God.*

focused less on entertainment and more on empowerment of their children? What if they were commissioned in the manner of Acts 1:8? Nothing in that powerful passage would indicate the exclusion of the young.

Kingdom Key #11

Are you too intellectual, too sophisticated to trust God like a little child? The Kingdom of God belongs to such as these and if we are to walk in his anointing, we must walk humbly.

Truly I tell you, anyone who will not receive the kingdom of God like a little child will never enter it.
Luke 18:17 (NIV)

Rosie

It's every parent's nightmare, bringing your newborn baby into this world with a physical defect.

Our third daughter, Rosie, had barely reached Belen's arms when she saw the large boil on her head. Boils can be treated, but her collarbone, protruding out as if broken, caused us both great concern.

Giving birth at home in the slums, we knew we must take her to the hospital as soon as possible. Though we had no money for such a visit, we trusted that the Lord would provide.

Yet, something in our spirits resisted going right away. We sensed we were to wait until her dedication to the Lord.

In a scene reminiscent of *The Lion King*, I lifted Rosie's tiny body at the church altar, dedicating ourselves and our other two daughters to the Lord. In a short time after, Belen changed Rosie's diaper and discovered the boil gone and the collarbone perfect.

Rosie's healing was a great testimony of God's goodness to the people we lived among.

The Ministry of Reconciliation

The Gospel of Reconciliation begins at home, but was never intended to only remain there. It is a message of hope that we as believers have been commissioned to share.

Sri Lanka experienced, for 25 years, the horrors of civil war until 2009. Yet, in this period, our churches and church planting efforts prospered. Why? Because we believed in the Gospel of Reconciliation.

We, like the Apostle Paul, have not only been reconciled to God through Christ, but have received the "Ministry of Reconciliation."

Kingdom Key #12

We who are reconciled must become reconcilers.

All this is from God, who reconciled us to himself through Christ and

gave us the ministry of reconciliation.
2 Corinthians 5:18 (NIV)

We must live out the truth Charles Wesley wrote so many years ago that we sing every Christmas:

Peace on earth and mercy mild, God and sinners reconciled...[1]

In this world of deep turmoil, God's chosen agents of reconciliation must be ready to act. That is, you and me – everyone who has spent time at the foot of the cross and experienced the glorious fact that God does not count their sin against them.

Each day presents an opportunity to be such an agent of change. If you ask, you'll be pleased how the Holy Spirit will give you "ears to hear and eyes to see" in the lives of people you encounter every day.

Once you begin to move in the ministry, you'll be surprised to find how much we as human beings are interconnected. Our physical self is connected to our soul, which is connected to our mind. When one part is suffering, others are impacted. That is why Jesus referred to us as a whole being when he commanded us to love God. He knew the most powerful of emotions could not be isolated from parts of ourselves.

"You shall love the Lord your God with all your heart, with all your soul, with all your strength, and with all your mind . . ."
Luke 10:27a (NKJV)

Of course, the second part of this verse is also critical in the ministry of reconciliation:

". . . and your neighbor as yourself." Luke 10:27b (NKJV)

Reconciliation can involve much more than restored relationships. Reconciliation initiated by the Holy Spirit can heal the mind, the soul, and even the body.

> **If you ask, you'll be pleased how the Holy Spirit will give you "ears to hear and eyes to see" in the lives of people you encounter every day.**

The Ballerina

A 60-year-old woman dying of cancer came to my office. Looking at her emaciated body, it seemed as if she might have only weeks to live. As we talked about her condition and about

her life, I soon became distracted by a visual image in my mind –
a 16-year-old girl, beautifully dancing like a ballerina, then,
suddenly stopping. I could see her face change from joy to
sadness in an instant.

The image was powerful enough to interrupt her to ask,
"What happened to you at age 16?"

She replied, "Nothing happened."

I wasn't convinced so I pressed in a bit, "Think about it please
and let me know."

She didn't hesitate to reply to my entreating, "No, nothing
happened."

We continued our conversation about her situation, but the
same images of a 16-year-old ballerina came to mind again. "I'm
so sorry, but are you sure nothing happened to you at age 16?"

"Yes, very sure," was her tart reply.

After this exchange, I thought I blew it. Maybe something
was distracting me. So we continued to share. But the ballerina
returned. "I'm so sorry, but I'm compelled to ask you again."

"No, Pastor!" she cut me off before I could continue.

Not wanting to continue a futile conversation, I said to her,
"Let's pray."

Maybe she knew that in prayer the Spirit would reveal the truth. She blurted out, "Yes, Pastor, yes!" and then tearfully began a story of suppressed pain.

At age 16, her brother tried to sexually abuse her, but she was able to stop him. Telling her mother only deepened the tragedy. Her mother became angry, accusing her of lying. If she told her father, he would kill her brother.

So she did what so many victims of sexual abuse do – they hide it in their hearts. It often grows like a disease with tentacles into the mind, the soul, and even the body.

Then a word of wisdom came to me and I shared it with her. "The reason God showed me this image is that he wants to heal you." The first part of this word, however, was dependent on her response to the second. "But not if you don't forgive your brother and your mother."

The Lord, of course, could heal her body, but it was her soul that was filled with the cancer of unforgiveness and hate.

She protested with every fiber of her weakened body, "I can't. I won't!"

Unraveling the web of pain spun by years of rejection is never easy. She would not find her healing unless she released her hurt.

In the next few moments she took the most courageous steps and forgave her brother and mother.

A week later she returned, completely healed of cancer.

Is cancer always related to a sin we've committed, or committed against us? Of course not, but the servant of the Lord must be able to move in the anointing of God's discernment to perceive the truth and entrust the rest to the Lord.

I've prayed for hundreds where the Lord revealed a deep bitterness that was connected to their affliction. He gave them the opportunity of experiencing not only freedom from the physical pain, but also freedom from the emotional pain. Sometimes they choose neither. One particular woman's words as she stood at the altar are haunting in their stubbornness, "I'd rather not be healed than to forgive."

Yet we are called to be ministers of reconciliation, whether people want it or not. We must be open to the Spirit's leading to see all of the ramifications of an unreconciled life. People are individually complex, interconnected beings that we unfortunately prefer to separate and compartmentalize. We can do the

"Reconciliation is desperately needed for the world we live in.

same when it comes to those same people living in community. Reconciliation is desperately needed for the world we live in.

Grave Diggers

The pastor, surrounded by armed men, absorbed blow after blow. They spared him only because they wanted one last thing from him. He joined others facing a similar fate and stumbled along into the jungle until ordered to stop.

Given a shovel, commanded to dig, he knew instantly that the next few minutes would be his last. What goes through one's mind when you are digging your own grave?

The high-pitched voices of terrorists screaming orders to dig faster joined the sounds of shovels penetrating the dirt. Both drowned out any whimpers from fear or pain. But another sound, barely heard in the distance, invaded the soon to be execution.

The whirling helicopter blades brought hope that help could be on the way. The Sri Lankan Airforce soon saved this pastor and the other hostages.

A month following, many in this group attended our Foursquare Convention. Most were recovering from broken bones inflicted by the terrorists. All were healed after prayer. But it would take a giant wave to test if their minds and hearts found similar recovery.

The Tsunami

Any day after Christmas is usually one of rest and recovery from holiday travels and big meals. This day after would prove very different. A 9.0 magnitude earthquake would hit off the coast of Sumatra. Waves of biblical proportion would crush the coasts of 14 nations, including my homeland, especially in that same region known for its terrorists.

The pastor and the others that had been terrorized and beaten were some of the first responders to this devastated area. They served, opening their homes and loving the families of terrorists, even some of the would-be-murderers themselves.

All of this while most terrorist leaders fled and the local temples' doors slammed. Those who had been once reconciled to Christ brought reconciliation to others in real, tangible ways – others who didn't deserve it. But isn't that the point? None of us do. Being saved means knowing you've received the most undeserved gift ever, and to hide that gift, not to share it in words and deeds, is the most selfish of acts.

After four months of this outpouring of selfless love, even the very people responsible for the beatings wanted to meet me. "None of our leaders helped us. But during our helplessness you opened your homes and your hearts."

They continued in this effusive praise of our servant leaders, "You are gods, we should worship you. You have something we don't have. Your God must be the true God!"

Reconciliation had come full circle. We shared with them why we served, why we loved, "If you want to be like us, worship our God."

Because of the efforts of Christians serving in the affected areas, thousands of people found Christ. They found him because they saw him in us. And the truth is, we also saw him in them. We are all God's children after all.

Kingdom Key #13

Look for opportunities to lavish unconditional love in impossible situations, and you'll experience radical reconciliation.

...And I pray that you, being rooted and established
in love, may have power...
to grasp how wide and long and high and deep is
the love of Christ, and to know this
love that surpasses knowledge—
that you may be filled to the measure
of all the fullness of God.
Ephesians 3:17-19 (NIV)

*D*ear Lord, you came into this world bearing a message of
reconciliation. You came to reconcile us with your Father.
Now, reconciled to the Father we are your children. Dear
Lord, teach us to forgive one another, cause our hearts to melt
and let the hardness of our hearts melt by your love. As much as
you forgave us, help us to forgive one another and be reconciled
to each other. Dear Lord, now that you have given us the
ministry and the message of reconciliation, please empower us
and grace us to reconcile others who are against one another.

Dear Lord, remove all divisions and animosities in this world and enable us to be peacemakers. In Jesus' name I release the ministry of reconciliation to you in this very moment.

4

THE GOSPEL OF RE-AWAKENING

One of my heroes in the faith, the late John Wimber, in his classic book *Power Evangelism*, begins the story:

"In 1982, Siripala and Winefreda, a middle-aged couple living in the Summitpura slums of Colombo, had an infant son who grew very ill. The worried parents called on Christian friends for help, but when they arrived, the child was dead."[1]

I love naps…when I can take them. They are rare, and when they come it better be important to be awakened out of one. So when the young pastor, he himself healed from deafness, came knocking on my door, we both knew it better be worthy. It was.

"Pastor, a boy who is very ill, he is dying. Please pray for him." It may sound heartless to say, but where we lived, death surrounded us constantly. It was more the urgency in his voice and the fact that I was mentoring him that I got quickly out of bed.

The family with the dying boy lived across town, some 12 miles away. With no money for an entire bus fare, we began to walk. When we arrived, this tiny little house was filled with people, inside and out. It looked more like a service before a funeral. I didn't know it then, but it was.

Seeing the baby lying on a cot, I immediately made my way over to him, lifting him up, holding his slumped head level to mine.

"I rebuke sickness, I rebuke disease, I rebuke death in Jesus' name!" And I said it all very loud.

The baby sneezed, then he began to cry. I handed him to the startled mother, Winefreda. Feeling bad that I had wakened a sleeping baby, I apologized to her.

"Pastor, he was dead!"

The boy had been dead for several hours, but I didn't know that when I arrived. If I had, I never would have picked him up from the cot.

Almost all of the 40 plus people who had witnessed this miracle gave their hearts to Christ after I shared the gospel – nothing like a "raising from the dead" to enhance the evangelism process.

Raising from the Dead – Part 2

While in the midst of an interview for visa in the Croatian consulate in Colombo, a co-worker called me on my phone. Barely able to express himself, he let me know his situation. In his arms, in the hospital, he held his dead child. Being a father of three beautiful children, I could hardly imagine his grief.

Being in the interview, too far away to come and console my friend, I prayed over the phone for his baby. "I speak life! I rebuke death!"

And then I hung up.

A few hours later, the father called me back. His first question, "Why did you hang up?" Before I could reply with my lame excuses, he proceeded to tell me that immediately after the prayer, the baby started screaming. He raced his child back to the doctor who had

"Nothing like a "raising from the dead" to enhance the evangelism process.

pronounced him dead minutes before. The doctor couldn't believe what he saw.

After that, I tried to be more careful when hanging up on a phone call.

The Gospel of Re-Awakening

I started this chapter with two stories of individual resurrection on purpose. As powerful a testimony of a life coming back from death – even more powerful an entire village or city emerging from the shadow of death to resurrection.

The same gospel that has the power to re-awaken the body from the dead can re-awaken a community. If we truly believe this, it impacts our vision, our focus, and our strategies to fulfill the Great Commission. To put it bluntly, we really believe God can do it.

"Go ye therefore, and teach all nations, baptizing them in the name of the Father, and of the Son, and of the Holy Ghost."
Matthew 28:19 (KJV)

What were Jesus' words just before his commissioning?

"All power is given unto me in heaven and in earth."
Matthew 28:18 (KJV)

Again, Paul's seminal words in his letter for the church in Philippi:

"That I may know him, and the power of his resurrection, and the fellowship of his sufferings, being made conformable unto his death." Philippians 3:10 (KJV)

Prayer and revival expert, the late, great Leonard Ravenhill, brilliantly summed up this verse with the following:

"Calvary expresses the love of God. The resurrection explains the power of God."[2]

The Gospel of Re-Awakening when applied to groups of people is an application of both Calvary and the resurrection. It is the gospel of love and of power joined together to demonstrate the character of God.

In Sri Lanka, we saw it occur when the gospel came in love and power to the Sinhalese and Tamils, devastated by war and the tsunami. Our efforts to rebuild homes, schools, community centers, and the digging of wells forced those of other faiths to reconsider prejudices regarding Christians. It was as if one hand lifting up the wounded stranger, while the other one held the Bible. Its words could now be heard with an open heart.

We firmly believed in the power of the resurrection and the fellowship of the sufferings. When working together there is no more powerful force or testimony of God's love. All that is needed are willing participants.

Kingdom Key #14

The leader who wants to move in God's anointing must be able and willing to move in his power and fellowship with those who need it most. They must be willing to be commissioned into an army that may go into any and every people group – across all social, economic, and racial lines.

There is neither Jew nor Greek, there is neither slave nor free, there is neither male nor female; for you are all one in Christ Jesus.
Galatians 3:28 (NKJV)

The Last Shall be First

Just after I graduated from Bible College in the Philippines, I was invited to be the senior pastor of a good-sized church in the capitol city of Colombo, Sri Lanka.

I could return home with my new bride and live a nice comfortable life. We would have children, take care of my parents, and live the abundant life Jesus promised. Elation, however, began to give way to fear and intimidation. Belen and I sought the Lord.

If you will allow me a brief moment to write to those young and new to pastoring before completing my story –

Dear Young Leader,

First, expect that you'll be tested regarding your motives. Why are you in ministry? Is it to be noticed? To fill a deep need to be loved? Is ministry success, the growth in size of the group you lead, the ultimate sign of God's anointing on your life? Are you open to God leading you to pastor a small, poor congregation? Are you more concerned about receiving the recognition of peers than representing the person of Jesus Christ?

Second, please ask these and even more penetrating questions of yourself because as you grow older in ministry, guess what? These questions only get magnified. And we can become less open to meaningful Spirit-led self-examination.

And third, don't completely trust your own introspection. Submit yourself and your ministry to those you believe will speak to you honestly and freely.

"Submit to one another out of reverence for Christ."

Ephesians 5:21 (NIV)

Do it now, young man or woman. Do it now before you walk down from a pulpit 20 years later wondering why you are preaching and realizing you missed God's real purpose for your life.

Sounds rough?

The ministry is rough. The dropout/burnout rates of pastors are depressing. Truly living out the gospel can be rough too. I love the admonition of Jesus:

"In the world you will have tribulation; but be of good cheer, I have overcome the world." John 16:33 (NKJV)

I admire the story of Matthew Barnett, son of a famous pastor, moving as a very young man to pastor in Los Angeles. At 20 years old, his first church, in a rough neighborhood among the poor and hopeless. With no ministry experience he wanted to become more a part of the

community in which he lived, so he did the unthinkable –
he moved his desk out of the office and onto the sidewalk. It
was the beginning act from a servant's heart that would
become an expansive ministry, eventually taking over an
empty hospital building and touching thousands of lives
with multiple ministries. Today, the Dream Center and
Angelus Temple have literally changed their community –
the power of the gospel to re-awaken.

I'm sure if you asked him, Pastor Matthew early on asked
himself some of the questions I'm asking you. And, like me,
I'm sure he still does.

Belen and I sought the word from the Lord. Should we
accept this generous position in Colombo, or did the Lord have
other plans? I didn't want my fears or sense of intimidation to
stop us from God's best.

As he always does, if we will listen, he spoke clearly. As the
congregation would grow in maturity, so would I. The established
church in Colombo would not give me the opportunity, but
planting a new church could. We would grow together.

Once that critical decision was settled, the next one involved
the location of this pioneer work. This, too, needed a clear answer

from the Lord. After serious prayer and fasting, our location emerged, Summitpura.

When the government hosted the non-aligned nations summit in the early seventies, they cleaned up the slums by the side of the main airport road which led to Colombo. This "clean up" meant thousands of homes destroyed and families displaced into a large area nick-named Summitpura.

In this region, one of the darkest places on earth, we began our church. It is difficult to describe the wickedness I saw as I prayer-walked through the streets. When the human spirit is broken, utterly without hope, it will be filled with everything that flesh can acquire.

Belen and I fasted for three weeks before I took my first prayer walk, intentionally leaving Belen behind. After the first day in the slums, I never wanted to return.

This is an assault on all your senses, physical, emotional, and spiritual, that few people have experienced. I wouldn't wish it on anyone – smells that invade your lungs, taking away breath, sights that enter your vision so horrifying you freeze in disbelief, sounds of combined cries, screams, and

"After the first day in the slums, I never wanted to return.

moans with street chatter, music, and honking horns. Together, they battle your soul.

There literally is nothing one can do in such a situation but pray. You must pray over your fears. Pray over the demonic strongholds. Pray over the pain that surrounds you. I prayed in the language of the Holy Spirit most of the time because, frankly, I did not know how to pray.

However, each day that I walked and prayed in tongues, I felt a growing strength, an increased inspiration to continue. By the seventh day, suddenly I sensed the ministry would begin. I felt that I should look for someone to share the gospel. It would be a day of re-awakening for a young man and the beginning of re-awakening for a city in darkness. I write of this more in the beginning of Chapter 6.

Kingdom Key #15

The person desiring to move in the anointing must seek the gifts of the Holy Spirit.

Now eagerly desire the greater gifts.
1 Corinthians 12:31 (NIV)

A Nation in Conflict

Though the armed civil conflict between Tamil rebels and Sri Lankan armed forces ended May of 2009, a death toll of possibly 70,000 left a nation in continued ethnic conflict. The Church rose to the challenge of building a bridge of reconciliation between the Sinhalese and Tamil people.

The Biblical solution to this division was and is the person of Jesus Christ. And it is his love that compels his body to respond in kind to bring Shalom. For me, it began one morning in July of 1983, leading devotions as the chaplain of the Colombo YMCA.

The words "When I survey the wondrous cross" filled the room of worshiping young men, but it was the noise of chaos outside that filled their minds. The crash of broken windows and screams for help were occurring just outside our building.

Mobs of angry people were assaulting a helpless minority. They were seeking revenge from reports of 13 soldiers killed by Tamil rebels in the North. The riots continued for days with about 3,000 Tamils killed and a hundred thousand forced to enter refugee camps after their homes were destroyed and businesses burned.

I watched as even children joined in on the assault, stopping vehicles and setting them on fire – with people inside. "Black July," as it would be called, would spiral into a civil war. Deeply impacted, Belen and I knew we must respond in the opposite spirit, the spirit of love.

Four Steps

Our first step was to add a new dimension to our church's ministry of evangelism and church planting: Encourage Sinhalese Christians to reach out to traumatized Tamils in refugee camps.

I also challenged each member of the YMCA to give of new clothes, shoes, food, and finances. The Sinhalese Christians were moved by the emotions expressed by the Tamil people. It encouraged us to continue the work of compassion.

Our second step was to visit all the places where innocent blood was shed and to repent. I taught how Cain was cursed for the shedding of his brother Abel's blood (Genesis 4:1-15). Soon, both Sinhalese and Tamil believers were united in prayer, asking God's forgiveness for their collective sin and to heal Sri Lanka. Leaders traveled from city to city, village to village, sharing the message of repentance and forgiveness.

The third step involved holding meetings among both people groups, not only in our Foursquare churches, but also across denominational lines. Two scriptures were our foundation for re-awakening our love for each other:

"Now all things are of God, who has reconciled us to Himself through Jesus Christ, and has given us the ministry of reconciliation, that is, that God was in Christ reconciling the world to Himself, not imputing their trespasses to them, and has committed to us the word of reconciliation." 2 Corinthians 5:18-19 (NKJV)

"For He Himself is our peace, who has made both one, and has broken down the middle wall of separation, having abolished in His flesh the enmity, that is, the law of commandments contained in ordinances, so as to create in Himself one new man from the two, thus making peace." Ephesians 2:14-15 (NKJV)

The pastors admonished one another to forgive, shed our ethnic differences, and begin to listen to each other.

To see Tamils and Sinhalese praying for each other gave all of us hope. Then, to see each group washing the other's feet, and then serving communion, brought a unity that words fail to describe.

Finally, our fourth course of action was the Sinhalese Christians' outreach to the Tamil people in the north and east, devastated by the tsunami. This was the other hand of the gospel, the gospel of love through action that brought real reconciliation.

These types of meetings continued through the civil war. For 27 years we came together as one. I believe the power of the gospel to bring us together was instrumental in the peace that eventually came and is sustained to this day.

I often think about the Palestinian people and Jewish people, how they so desperately need a similar course of action. But,

> *"The pastors admonished one another to forgive, shed our ethnic differences, and begin to listen to each other.*

one can name dozens of conflicts in every nation that cry out for a Gospel of Re-Awakening.

Fruit that Remains

As of my writing, our Foursquare churches and others continue to be involved with many projects that demonstrate the character of God.

There are several thousand children who lost both of their parents as a result of the tsunami and war. Our churches run two children's homes in the Tamil-speaking cities of Jaffna and Trincomalee. We have one more children's home in Colombo in which we have both Sinhalese and Tamil children growing together. Nothing is more rewarding than seeing these children embrace each other and knowing they are the hope of the new generation.

The need to help these children far outweighed our two homes, so we launched a foster care program. This program plus a school to help children with disabilities, a home for teenage girls, a center for young widows, and another for older widows, continues to thrive.

For years, we organized a series of medical camps among tsunami and war refugees – helping tens of thousands of victims. These camps also experienced great moments of reconciliation.

Our Vocational Training Institute in Vavuniya was established close to our Teen Rehabilitation Center to provide training for the girls. They are trained in various vocational arts to provide careers once they leave.

Another similar project called The Dorcas Project provides vocational training for young widows, teaching them to support themselves and their children.

Besides building over 100 homes for tsunami victims, we have partnered with the Sri Lanka Army to build water wells among the resettled Tamil refugees.

Our churches continue to meet needs that their communities face. It may be purchasing computers for schools or helping the police with office furniture or blood drives.

Final Thoughts

To spread the Gospel of Re-Awakening, the church must understand that it lives not in a vacuum, but in a community often made up of cultures and sub-cultures.

The church and its leaders must be willing to do the hard work of identifying its neighbors – looking beyond the superficial and into the heart of each culture.

We must, as agents of reconciliation, find where we can bring Shalom. We must believe that our presence brings the presence of Christ, hence, peace.

In America, this multi-cultural nation has a unique challenge as a country

> *"To spread the Gospel of Re-Awakening, the church must understand that it lives not in a vacuum, but in a community often made up of cultures and sub-cultures.*

founded by immigrants who eventually subdued by arms the various native cultures. Add to that the forced immigration of slaves from Africa, indentured servants from Asia and Europe, and you have a country still grappling with issues of race and reconciliation.

The Church in the U.S. that believes in repentance and salvation in Jesus Christ must be the leading agent of dialogue. It cannot and must not hide behind its stained glass windows. If 11:00 a.m. on Sunday morning continues to be the most segregated time of the week, it will have missed a powerful moment of global transformation. How?

America exports, via Hollywood, much in the way of culture, good and bad. I believe that an America that heals its racial wounds through the two hands of the gospel will also impact the world.

But first, the local churches must believe in the power of the gospel to affect real change. Like the person resurrected from the dead, entire communities wrapped in the grave cloth of prejudice and hate can walk together out of the grave.

We are living it here in Sri Lanka, though not perfect or complete. I believe it can happen in the U.S. and around the world where the church rises up to its God-given place, demonstrating the true character of our Lord Jesus Christ.

Just as I rebuked sickness and death from the dead baby, can we not together rebuke with word and deed the sins that separate us? And, must we not expect the same power of God to bring a re-awakening?

I pray it so.

Dear Lord, I pray that you awaken us to your great love. May we repent and return to our first love. I

pray for ourselves that we would experience spiritual resuscitation from our spiritual death and coldness. Set us on fire today; re-awaken us anew to your great renewal of faith and prayer. Dear Lord, I pray that you would re-awaken everyone who reads this book to great possibilities and amazing lives of victory each day. I release upon you a Holy Ghost revival and re-awakening, in Jesus' name, amen.

5

THE GOSPEL OF
SHALOM

S ometimes the Gospel of Peace comes in the most
unexpected ways in the most unexpected situations.
In Sri Lanka, a home invasion robbery may involve a four-ton
perpetrator, and usually all they steal is salt. However, despite
the docile images of elephants in zoos, the wild Asian
Elephants in my country are often lethal when they invade a
village looking for their favorite condiment.

One such encounter occurred to a new believer, a 40-year-
old woman who was instructed after her conversion to face any
type of challenge by calling on the name of Jesus. The pastor
left her with the proclamation, "He is a miracle-working God!"

She would soon find out just how valuable those instructions were.

Shopping for food in the local outdoor market, her walk home was interrupted by not one, but ten elephants, completely surrounding her. Agitated and probably hungry, the elephants swayed and stomped, raising their massive trunks to roar disapproval.

The poor woman, remembering the pastor's words, fell to her knees and cried out simply, "Jesus!" She repeated his name over and over again until one by one the elephants left her unscathed and praising God.

The name of Jesus changes the very atmosphere in any situation. It brings peace in times of panic.

Since we're on the elephant subject…

Alleluia

One of our pastors, sent to plant a church in a rural part of north/central Sri Lanka, started in a home with some 15 people. He challenged each to witness their faith to someone and to invite them to the next meeting.

One of the attendees, taking the pastor up on the challenge, found someone to share with – a poor, uneducated woman, looking hopeless. This older woman, beaten repeatedly by her drunken husband, eagerly received the invitation to the next meeting and the promise of "when we pray, problems are solved and peace will come."

Unfortunately, the woman did not understand any of the teaching from the meeting. She did come away, however, with a one-word song, *Alleluia*. She sang it over and over. Each time brought more and more peace and lifted her depression. But the test of her newfound "peace" had yet to walk through her door.

She heard the normal noises produced from her husband's stupefied stumble into their tiny home – so inebriated that he fell on their bed asleep. She was spared the usual beating. At 2:00 in the morning, the noise of branches being broken in their thatched roof startled her. But what caused her to panic? A huge elephant trunk, protruding through the coconut leaves, in search of salt.

Elephants can literally crush a house and kill everyone inside in their frenzied hunt for food. Her screams were justified and quickly sobered up her husband.

But the test of her newfound "peace" had yet to walk through her door.

In the moment, all she could think to do was to shout, "Alleluia! Alleluia!" (Interestingly enough, the Sinhalese word for elephant is *allieya*.) As soon as she repeated the word a few times, the elephant pulled its trunk out, in terror, and ran away.

Her husband, in disbelief of the elephant's uncharacteristic response, asked her, "When did you learn the Elephant Language?"

The poor woman wondered herself. Maybe they did teach her the "Elephant Language." So she asked her husband if he'd like to go with her next time to learn this language too.

Completely sober, he went with his wife to the next meeting. With a bit more education and understanding, he fully grasped the gospel and explained it to his wife. Both received Christ.

The Gospel of Shalom entered their very hard life in the most unconventional way.

Shalom

Peace is a highly prized commodity in cultures that experience a constant interplay between superstition and fear. In Sri Lanka, a certain type of bird flying over your house, making a particular noise, is a very bad omen. To the superstitious, it means certain death in the family and the immediate need to search out the help of a witchdoctor or priest. And this type of reaction is not merely for the uneducated. Politicians and powerful business people also fall under the spells.

In the West, people lack peace sometimes due to their own cultural superstitions, but more often because of fears of the unknown. How many people do you know who lack peace in their lives because of the fear of finances, health, and even the after-life?

Our world is desperate for peace – not the transitory peace culture displays from its commercial windows, but relational peace from the Prince of Peace. Unfortunately, even believers have failed to grasp and experience the deeper level of peace offered by Jesus.

Peace was not, in Jesus' view, a passive state of mind. It wasn't merely a "state of consciousness" or a place devoid of conflict. Jesus, a Jew, used the word understanding its fuller meaning in the Hebrew root: to restore, bring wholeness, completeness, well being, and harmony.

Peace, and the act of taking it into situations, was a part of Jesus' commission to his followers. It's *shalom* that he speaks to his disciples to take into any home that would receive them, and that same shalom, which he would speak over fearful men doubting his resurrection.

It literally changed the atmosphere in the room.

> "*Our call as his disciples is to see broken lives restored, brought into harmony and wholeness, whenever we find them.*

To the woman who fell at his feet in tears, he commanded her to export the presence she had just encountered to others. "Go in peace."[1] Peace, shalom on this earth as it is in heaven, is as real and tangible as the alabaster jar she poured anointing oil from onto the Lord.

We are all called to pour out the anointing oil on others. Like the woman, we must spend intimate time with Jesus, not merely for the experience of joy and peace, but to take that peace to a fearful world.

Our call as his disciples is to see broken lives restored, brought into harmony and wholeness, whenever we find them.

Kingdom Key #16

The anointing begins and ends with a desire and deep hunger to be filled with his presence that emanates a peace that brings the Kingdom on earth as it is in heaven.

…my peace I give unto you: not as the world giveth, give I unto you…John 14:27 (KJV)

The Good Witchdoctor

"I'm a good witchdoctor!" the man proclaimed, sitting across from me in my office. He spoke the truth; he was by all indication a good and decent man.

He had fallen on hard times. His business of selling "medicine" to clients was losing money. He made his concoctions boiling roots he dug up after being directed by spirits. They would tell him what trees to go to, exact roots to dig up, and how much to boil. As evil as the practice was, his motives were to genuinely help people – a rarity among the many witchdoctors I've encountered.

He started matter-of-factly again, "I'm a good witchdoctor. I heal people by the spirits."

I shared with him the gospel and made him promise never to contact the spirits again.

"Yes, I promise. I'm so tired."

We proceeded through a time of repentance and renouncing, breaking curses and casting out demons. He was totally delivered, experiencing real peace for the first time. Then he asked me something that took me by surprise, "I want to learn the language you were speaking. Did you learn it overseas? I want to know it."

I realized he was referring to my speaking in tongues.

"Whenever you spoke that language, I could feel demons leave me. I felt lighter each time you spoke it."

I could see the sincerity in his face.

"Please train me on this."

Gladly, I prayed for him to be filled in the Holy Spirit and to speak in tongues. Ten minutes prior, filled with spirits – now filled in the Holy Spirit. Peace had come to his household.

Kingdom Key #17

Moving in shalom will expose you to the kingdom of darkness. The peace of God comes with you into the hidden places. Be prepared for a power encounter, always remembering:

…greater is he that is in you, than he that is in the world. 1 John 4:4 (KJV)

The Passport

Once, in Singapore, I visited the Sri Lankan Embassy to renew my passport. I knew this wouldn't be an easy experience, but didn't expect my encounter with the first official.

"No, that can't happen," he said, shaking his head in the negative.

If you travel as much as I do, red stop signs are really only flashing yellow "slow down" signs. You can never give up on the first "no." Plus, being a child of the most-high God has its advantages. So I appealed to the Deputy High Commissioner.

When I walked into his office, he seemed to be stunned. What I told him next really threw him off. "I want to tell you something God spoke to me about you and your family." I let that sink in then added, "But not here in your office."

By the way, like the TV ads say, "Don't try this at home." You better "know that you know" and have plenty of experience listening to the voice of the Lord before exercising a "word" on a government official – especially one who can ban you permanently from your home!

"Can I meet you tomorrow evening?" he asked, a little more than curious. I agreed, under the condition he would bring my passport.

I had told him where I was staying and he arrived promptly. I didn't want to waste his time or mine, so I shared soon after exchanging greetings.

I went into details of his health, both physically and mentally. I moved into challenges in his office and the needs in his family, especially a son walking in rebellion – the same son he brought with him to meet me. The details were such that he knew that either God talked to me or I was a government spy.

He trusted I represented God. Laying hands on both they fell backward, flat on the ground, under the power of the Holy Spirit. What he told me once he recovered is descriptive of how shalom can enter any space where a person of peace enters. "I would not have come here tonight except for the feeling I had in your presence. It was so good, so calming."

Grateful for the amazing encounter he had with God, he gave me my new passport.

> "*The details were such that he knew that either God talked to me or I was a government spy.*

Shalom Community

"In the final analysis, we are not called to build bigger or better churches...We as the church are to focus on working for the realization of the shalom community in our political, economic, and religious life together." – Robert Linthicum, *Transforming Power*[2]

Shalom community is one in which Jesus Christ is Lord, who has broken down the wall that has caused human beings to function as strangers to one another. Shalom is a community in which all human divisions that alienate and separate people from one another through race, color, ethnicity, language, gender, wealth, education, and power are eradicated.

Such a community is possible when we allow God's love and power to transform our lives and mindsets. Christians are called to live intentionally, looking for opportunities to sow seeds of peace.

How? First, Christians need to walk in peace and in so doing affect the atmosphere of a nation with the presence of God. We live in a time of much anger and discord. Believers must model the spirit of peace just as they follow the Prince of Peace. Leaders like Martin Luther King and Gandhi understood that no real change can happen unless the heart of man changes first. And to see that change, an angry person must witness the man of peace.

Second, the believer can impact the atmosphere by living a life obedient to the Word of God, bringing blessing to the city. Jeremiah, the prophet, spoke the Word of the Lord to exiles of Israel in Babylonian captivity encouraging them to prosper where they were planted.

"Seek the peace and prosperity of the city to which I have carried you into exile. Pray to the LORD for it, because if it prospers, you too will prosper." Jeremiah 29:7 (NIV)

Peace and prosperity come to a city when God's people pray. During the Colombo riots in July 1983, our churches were called to nationwide fasting and prayer. Before long, all the Christians in the city began to experience the Shalom of God.

The Man and Woman of Peace

The husband and wife strolled together, passed the park benches and hungry pigeons. Looking like any Middle Eastern, middle-aged, and middle class couple living in a strict Muslim nation, they went unnoticed.

But their walk in the park had purpose. They prayed as they passed by people, asking the Lord to lead them to the man or woman "of peace." They hoped to begin a series of conversations that would eventually lead to conversion.

Interestingly, these conversations normally never begin by talking about Jesus. In fact, one church planter in an extremely closed nation has said, "We don't introduce Jesus until he has introduced himself." His meaning? They only speak to people that the Lord is leading them to; and if the Lord is moving upon that person, the series of spiritual conversations will be used by the Spirit to ultimately reveal Jesus.

Peace sought out peace. The born-again couple, intimately familiar with the Prince of Peace, was on mission to find yet unsaved individuals where shalom hovered over, like the cloud covering the wandering children of Israel.

By the way, this couple and many others using this form of evangelism in dangerous areas spend hours in prayer and fasting. They have learned how to hear the Spirit's voice, and just as importantly, learned to respond with faith-filled action.

I can't be more specific due to high security concerns, but this type of witnessing is occurring in many closed to the gospel nations. It is a Spirit-led strategy of personal evangelism that is leading to the planting of thousands of underground churches. It follows the admonition and instructions Jesus gave to his disciples when he initially sent them out on their own.

"Now whatever city or town you enter, inquire who in it is worthy and stay there till you go out. And when you go into a household, greet it. If the household is worthy, let your peace come upon it. But if it is not worthy, let your peace return to you. And whoever will not receive you nor hear your words, when you depart from that house or city, shake off the dust from your feet."
Matthew 10:11-14 (NKJV)

In obscurity to the world but not the Kingdom of God, servants like this couple risk everything to seek out the lost. Coming in peace, they look to see where, or better, on whom shalom rests. If their words are not accepted, they will move on to another. If they are received, their peace will come upon the person listening.

It is what personal evangelism, no matter the circumstances, should always be – a Spirit-led, divine encounter.

We don't have to live under persecution to witness in a manner similar to the first followers of Jesus. We simply need to operate in a deeper understanding of shalom. Again, peace is not passive; it is active. Indeed, it is a fruit of the Spirit to be lived out in everyday life, yet it surpasses all human understanding. Like the woman who wept at Jesus' feet and dried them with her hair, we are all commissioned by our Lord to "go in peace." It is the call to the church today that unfortunately seems either misunderstood or simply ignored. Can you imagine a church excitedly exiting the pews, eager to bring shalom to their neighborhoods?

In the end, it is the church's call to experience "on earth, peace, goodwill toward men." As one author states,

"A primary responsibility of the church in the city is to seek the reconciliation and Shalom of its people."[3]

The Bomb

One morning while having breakfast with Belen, I had a vision — a disturbing vision. What I saw: the car of a minister in our government blow up.

The vision was strong and clear enough that I felt compelled to contact their office and see if I could share it. I described the vision to this minister's assistant and asked, "Do you think the minister would want to talk with me?"

"Yes, we will send a car."

Not having all the details of the vision revealed to me, I replied, "No thanks, I will drive myself."

The dignified individual graciously greeted me, anxious to hear my story. After sharing the details of the car bombing, I pronounced that it would occur in three days.

Their reply, "Is there any hope for me?"

"*Bring peace wherever God plants you, knowing you are a part of a larger community committed to bringing it "to earth as it is in heaven."*

"Yes, you will be protected if you give your heart to Jesus."

It didn't take any more convincing for the minister to pray with me.

Within the next three days, it was discovered that an aide to this government official confessed to attempting to bomb the car with the minister inside. Needless to say, the minister was grateful.

Bring peace wherever God plants you, knowing you are a part of a larger community committed to bringing it "to earth as it is in heaven."

*D*ear Lord, you said in John 14:27, "Peace I leave with you, my peace I give to you; not as the world gives do I give to you. Let not your heart be troubled, neither let it be afraid." Your peace fills the earth and fills the hearts that live for you and glorify your name. Your shalom is health, wealth, fruitfulness, tranquility, and everything wholesome and good. I pray that we your people be brought into your grace of shalom. I release through prayer God's shalom on you, in Jesus' name.

6

THE GOSPEL OF TRANSFORMATION

"The Spirit of the Lord is upon me, because He anointed me to preach the gospel to the poor." Luke 4:18a (NASB)

The street, narrow and muddy, still drying from the monsoon season, lined with buildings peeling faded paint of greens and blues.

Clotheslines holding red and orange saris, baking in a still heat. Children, shoeless, shirtless, jumping over puddles, splashing gold clay against their dark skin.

Young women leaning inside doorways, trying to catch my eye, hoping I will be their next customer. Young men slump against walls, weakened by the poison of drugs and alcohol pumping through their blood.

This is my church and I pray for my congregation. Their lives will be transformed though none know it yet.

Beginnings

Now in my second week after returning to Colombo from Bible school in the Philippines, I pride myself in growing a bit wiser than my first week.

I spot the pickpockets, though they would find my pockets lacking, and I can recognize the face of someone who won't scream obscenities at me for sharing the gospel.

Armed with gospel tracts, useful to both share the message and use as a distraction if I need to flee, I pray with eyes wide open. My prayers lead me to a young man sitting and staring. Something about him looked even more hopeless than those around him. I decide to walk toward him.

Seeing my advance, he quickly flees into one of the many shacks that pressed against each other lining the streets. I sense God's heart so I enter this home only to hear the young man scream in terror.

The wounds that life can inflict on the very poor go way beyond economic deprivation. I try not to imagine why he screamed, what memories he experienced in that moment of time. Fortunately, his mother seems to calm him as she places herself between her troubled son and me. "What do you want?"

I realize I need to get right to the point. "I want to pray for his healing." By then, hearing his screams and guttural sounds, I know he is a deaf mute.

The mother, though initially startled, puts her arm around her son to both comfort him and bring him closer to me. I lay my hands on his head and pray for his healing. I could feel the power of God flow from my hands into this young man's body.

I spend the next few minutes watching him speak for the very first time, exchanging words with his mother, who occasionally glanced back at me. He would later become a pastor of one of our churches.

This would be the first of dozens of miracles that would take place in the streets and homes of the "least of these." Like the first church, signs and wonders would be instrumental in

> *I could feel the power of God flow from my hands into this young man's body.*

growing the church in the slums. Our churches would be homes filled with new believers, seekers, and the curious.

Our church planting strategy was simple: preach the Good News, demonstrate the power of God, watch evil flee, and see lives transformed.

"And do not be conformed to this world, but be transformed by the renewing of your mind, that you may prove what is that good and acceptable and perfect will of God." Romans 12:2 (NKJV)

Christianity was never intended to be only an individual pursuit. Many of us in the East find odd the concept of private religion.

Faith is meant to be lived out in community. Though we are all individual owners of our own relationship with God, the second half of the greatest commandment includes our neighborhood.

To put in terms my Western movie friends will best understand, in the Kingdom of God there are no "John Wayne Christians." No disrespect for the late, great actor intended. The gospel begins with you, but must always end with fulfilling the Great Commission.

And when disciples from every ethnic group are made and mobilized, the Kingdom of God will be established in every nation. This will have a natural impact on society, culture, government, business, and education. Quite the opposite of a misunderstanding of being "not of this world" – we are ambassadors of Christ[1], establishing the Kingdom in every profession. We are the light of the world, are we not?

Kingdom Key #18

The anointing is given to establish and demonstrate the Kingdom of God on earth just as Jesus did.

…God anointed Jesus of Nazareth with the Holy Spirit and with power, who went about doing good and healing all who were oppressed by the devil, for God was with Him.
Acts 10:38 (NKJV)

My good friend and fellow co-worker, Ted Olbrich, took over a fledgling church in Cambodia nearly two decades ago. He soon found the best way to extend the Kingdom in this nation, still suffering from genocide, was to serve the orphans and many widows.

Tens of thousands of orphans and converts later, members of the Foursquare Church in Cambodia fill some of the most influential roles in the marketplace. Doctors, lawyers, media people, and government officials owe their new destiny to the Lord, as introduced by the Olbrichs.

In Sri Lanka, a culture steeped in the traditional caste system, our converts circumvent the old ways to not only better their lives, but also impact the society around them.

Cambodia and Sri Lanka are similar in that our societies evolved in poverty, and the lack of government safety nets forces families and communities to depend on each other or die. It's natural for churches in such cultures to live in the fullness of community.

The Dream

In 1988, during a plane flight, I had a dream in which three well-dressed businessmen came to talk with me. Their questions were blunt and straightforward:

"Why haven't you come to us?"

"Why have you only gone to the poor?"

"We need the gospel as well."

This dream began much prayer for wisdom from the Lord to help us reach beyond the slums and into all strata of society. A turning point for our movement came a year later when we invited Dr. Jack Hayford to speak. His very presence gave our new work credibility among the other evangelical and Pentecostal churches. The depth of his teaching left hundreds of leaders wanting to grow in the Scriptures.

On his last day in our nation, Pastor Jack asked me a question, "What does the number 12 mean to you?" I instantly replied that it had been exactly 12 years since God had called me into the ministry.

He began to prophesy over me.

"After 12 years you have passed a milestone in your ministry and from this point on you will see a continual rise in

"Why have you only gone to the poor?

fruitfulness and blessing. The Foursquare movement is going to take a turn and things are going to explode in growth."

The very next Sunday, our English congregation of eight in Nugegoda grew to 40. This church not only continued to grow, but attracted many business people, becoming the key financial supporter of our nationwide effort.

As of my writing, we have over 1,800 churches and 530 pastors, of which the vast majority are in their 20s and 30s. 80% of our pastors and workers are first generation Christians, saved and trained through our movement.

Touching Nations

Our leaders who experienced transformation and moved to other nations often emerge in leadership in their new host country. They are amazing examples of the ability of the gospel to transcend any cultural and ethnic barrier.

The national leaders of the Foursquare Churches in the United Kingdom, New Zealand, Bahrain, and Dubai are from Sri Lanka.

Theo and Manju Nayagam were a young family Belen and I enjoyed discipling in Sri Lanka. We recognized early on that they were appointed by God to become "shepherds of shepherds." Eventually, they were sent to New Zealand as missionaries. A year later, in 2002, the Falkiner family, missionaries to Sri Lanka from Canada, joined them and together they planted the first Foursquare Church in East Auckland, New Zealand in 2003. Today, Theo serves as the National Leader that oversees 10 churches and 17 pastors.

KL and Yvonne Bhaskaran, born in Hindu families in Sri Lanka, took jobs in Bahrain where they grew in their faith and knowledge of the Lord. The growth of this wonderful family culminated in their pastoring a strong congregation that has eleven different nationalities. KL is also the National Leader of Bahrain and an observer on the Foursquare Global Council.

Surekha and Chrishani Hullugale took over a church Belen and I were pioneering in the early 1990s. As bi-vocational pastors, their church grew and prospered. A multi-national company offered him a transfer to London that they initially declined. But, after hearing an audible voice from the Lord and being given a word confirming the move, they moved and within a year took over as bi-vocational pastors of an existing Foursquare church. In 2011, they were appointed as National Leaders and have been instrumental in the healing and growth of the Foursquare work in the U.K.

Nixon Alexander, trained in our LIFE Bible Institute in Colombo, was offered employment in Dubai, United Arab Emirates where he was joined by his wife and children. When I visited in 2004, I shared a word from the Lord to plant a church. Not only did they do this faithfully and successfully, but they also planted three more churches. As the Foursquare National Leader of Dubai, Nixon oversees the Sri Lankan congregation and two Filipino churches.

Nothing offers Belen and me more satisfaction than to see how God is using these courageous families we've had the honor of sharing our lives with all around the globe. The Lord continues to whisper in our ears that there are many more to come.

The Bomber

A wonderful example of the gospel moving in power, transformation, and reconciliation happened among one of our churches overseas. Because of the still-sensitive nature of this testimony, I will need to leave out some of the specifics.

He was greatly feared in Sri Lanka. Trained in every aspect of military tactics, he never wavered in pulling the trigger. Many met their fate at the end of his rifle. However, after many years of dedicated service, honoring his parents' request to leave the battleground, he relocated to the U.K. Months of attempting to adjust to civilian life left him battling with alcohol and emotional trauma.

Feeling completely lost, he decided to become a suicide bomber and die a martyr for his cause. His sister, hearing of the news, visited him trying to discourage him from his mission. Exasperated, her final request to her brother: that they would go to church together for the very last time. He accepted her invitation.

They attended a mid-week evening prayer service where members would typically break into small groups and pray. Much to the horror of this man, he became separated from his sister. If the separation didn't cause enough anxiety, soon one in his prayer group, an African woman, began speaking in tongues for five straight minutes.

She spoke not in a prayer language, but in classical Tamil, one of the two main languages of Sri Lanka. Her message was the full gospel – words of invitation to Christ, words of love from Jesus himself. But they also included stories from the battlefield, how his life was spared, stories no one could possibly know. And this all took place in his native language.

He was deeply moved, especially when this sister concluded, "Why are you trying to destroy yourself?"

When the prayer time ended, he immediately addressed this obedient woman and asked how she knew his mother tongue.

> *There would be no more killing, for the gospel had set these captives free.*

"I don't know any Tamil," she rather incredulously replied.

The force of the moment nearly took his breath away. Only the true God could meet him in such a powerful way. He gave his troubled heart to Christ that evening, never leaving to fulfill his deadly mission. God had other plans.

Ironically, some three years later while sharing his testimony in church, someone in the audience approached him afterward. He too was ex-military from Sri Lanka, only on the opposite side. They knew each other with each hoping to kill the other.

There would be no more killing, for the gospel had set these captives free.

The Power of Transformation

"Therefore, if anyone is in Christ, the new creation has come: The old has gone, the new is here!" 2 Corinthians 5:17 (NIV)

One of the greatest proofs of the transformational nature of the gospel is its power to bring together ethnic groups that have clashed for decades.

Another fellow co-worker, Rev. Greg Fisher, now with Foursquare Missions Press, served as pastor in the aftermath of the horrible Rwandan genocide. His congregation in Kampala, Uganda was filled with ethnic Hutus and Tutsis, many who had slaughtered the family members of each other. Yet it was the power of the gospel to deeply transform hearts and minds that allowed them to worship together.

In Cambodia, missionary Ted Olbrich has churches with ex-Khmer Rouge leaders who butchered thousands of innocents. Yet, the gospel message transformed them, enabling each to be forgiven and to forgive themselves.

Sri Lanka's lengthy civil war created a simmering unrest even after the peace treaty was signed. Several thousands were killed during racial riots in 1983. Tamils would never think of entering a Sinhalese home and vice-versa.

Yet, our house churches are filled with living examples of people who have laid down old hate and have embraced each other in the name of Christ. The redemptive power of the gospel is playing a huge role in seeing nations experience real peace.

Kingdom Key #19

The person of God who wants to move in the anointing must desire to recognize and to willingly lay down old prejudices, wrongs, and hurts.

The anointing only operates in the truth of the Word, never self-delusion or deception, as the anointing from God transforms people, setting them free.

Then Jesus said to those Jews who believed Him, "If you abide in My word, you are My disciples indeed. And you shall know the truth, and the truth shall make you free."
John 8:31–32 (NKJV)

AIDS and the Church

During the height of the AIDS crises in the late 1980s, some preachers proclaimed it was the judgment of God upon the sin of homosexuality. Though many in the Evangelical/Pentecostal Church did not hold this view, their collective silence proved deafening. This posture only further alienated the Church from the homosexual community. While I had the joy of praying for two AIDS patients and seeing their healing, the need for a relational healing between two very different communities cried out.

According to one American pastor who ministered inside an AIDS hospice run by radical homosexual activists during this period, real dialogue and understanding was possible. Not only had he seen the lives of AIDS patients transformed by the gospel, but he also saw the potential for the Church and gay community to calm the growing hostilities.

"I didn't expect us all to hold hands and sing *Kumbaya*, but I did experience real heartfelt dialogue and actual breakthroughs of understanding."

This pastor went on to tell me, "But the reason they would listen to me is that I proved myself to them. They knew I backed up my words with love. Two years of volunteering every week at the hospice gave me the credibility to speak and to be heard—yet, never compromising my faith."

Sadly, only a couple of individuals would follow this pastor's example. And nationwide, even globally, the Church failed a great opportunity to display the unconditional love of God to a vulnerable and hurting community.

Today, the gulf between these communities seems beyond repair. If another transformational opportunity presents itself, will the Church be ready?

The transforming power of love to the marginalized, the hated, the vilified, must come from believers who when seeing the person dying from AIDS does not see a sinner, but sees Jesus.

> *"If another transformational opportunity presents itself, will the Church be ready?*

"When did we see you sick or in prison and visit you?"

"Truly, I say to you, as you did it to one of the least of these my brothers, you did it to me." Matthew 25:39-40 (ESV)

Dear Lord, your word in Romans 12:2 says that we should be transformed by the renewing of our minds. We need to be transformed in our thinking; our thought lives need to be completely changed that we might be able to think like Jesus, live like Jesus, and function as he functioned. Dear Lord, our prayer is that we would die to our old sin-loving natures and be transformed to live lives which glorify your name. I pray for you a release from the grips of sin, carnal indulgences, and addictions. I release you to be free to walk in the newness of life, transformed to live for God's glory. In Jesus' name, amen.

7

THE GOSPEL OF HIS RETURN

I was scared.

Her eyes always seemed to look beyond my own and into some chamber of my heart. Sensing my fear, she drew me close with a motion of her firm hand, then spoke softly into my ear. "Don't be afraid, Leslie. It's a good thing that he is coming back. For we will not only be judged, but transformed."

In my 12-year-old mind, words like judgment and transformation could stir a deep sense of awe. They still do. Jesus, the suffering savior of the world, according to my dear grandmother, could come back, a conquering king, at any time.

My fear turned to an overwhelming excitement. Time is short. People need to know. I must tell the world.

Some things never change.

As a teenager, I would frequently ask friends and strangers alike the question, "Are you ready?"

Even my three sisters, experiencing the same combination of fear and attraction I did in my grandmother's arms, gave their hearts to Christ after I asked the question and shared the gospel.

To this day, my heart warms with the expectation of Jesus' return. It's a part of my spiritual DNA. It's the fourth square of the Foursquare Gospel:[1]

The soon coming King!

If we believe this, it changes everything.

The late missiologist, J. Herbert Kane, once wrote that great leaders must have great energy for God.[2] What should give us all great energy, focus, and clarity of purpose is the coming of Christ. Whatever your eschatological position on the second coming, the bottom line is that he *is* coming and the age-old question remains:

Are You Ready?

Preparedness, Passion, and Purpose

One of my favorite stories about St. Francis of Assisi comes from his garden of beans. He was hoeing in his garden when approached by fellow monastics. Possibly irritated by his lack of urgency in ministry, they inquired, "Brother Francis, what would you do if you knew the world would end today?"

He calmly replied, "I suppose I would finish hoeing this row of beans."[3]

His message to his inquisitive friends was clear; I am prepared because I am in the perfect will of God.

The Second Coming inspires us to live every day as if he is returning, yet not at some frantic unsustainable pace. We should be living each 24 hours with both the emotional joy that we may meet him, and if we don't, we have pleased him with how we lived that day.

I've found that when I live a day with great excitement about his return, everything about that day seems to come alive – as if all my senses are heightened. The things of this world seem to, like the words of the old hymn, "grow strangely dim," and the prayer of Jesus "on earth as it is in heaven" explodes in my heart.

Kingdom Key #20

We will seek the anointing even more urgently when we expect his soon return. Live each day to its fullest as if he may be coming.

Watch therefore, for you know neither the day nor the hour in which the Son of Man is coming.
Matthew 25:13 (NKJV)

So how do we live as if Jesus is coming back today or tomorrow?

Like St. Francis of Assisi, live with such a consistency of a.) Courage b.) Character c.) Commitment that in your daily life you are prepared for that "great and terrible day" to come.

Courage

Courage is a broad term. Allow me to narrow it a bit to courage to live consistently in Kingdom life. As an Ambassador of Christ, you are called to represent his kingdom.

> *"So how do we live as if Jesus is coming back today or tomorrow?*

Until he comes again his kingdom will only be established by those he has chosen – you and me. He will grant us full armor and power in the Holy Spirit, but we must take the ground he puts before us. The enemy of our souls does not give up his territory lightly. He will fight us for every inch.

In Sri Lanka, demonic warfare is out in the open. Even the non-believers see it and tremble. In countries like America, one is less likely to experience such an encounter, but it does happen. For those of us used to this battle, the expressions of fear and lack of courage even among the spiritual elite is unfortunately too common.

Demons – American Style

I was asked to speak at one of the major churches in the United States. As often happens, a large line of people gather after my message to receive prayer. Even when I pray, I often keep my eyes open to see what the Spirit is doing. This time, my natural eyes caught an unusual sight.

A young man, possibly in his early thirties, kept getting in line then getting out of line. He repeated this a few times before finally allowing me to pray for him. As soon as I laid my hands on his head, he began to manifest demons. I immediately took authority, but he continued to writhe on the ground, cursing, thrashing.

The elders of the church attempted to restrain him, trying to allow me the opportunity to pray for those remaining in line while they concerned themselves with this young man. He was, as I learned later, a pastor in the church. The elders, however well intended, did not know what to do.

My first order of business was to address the elders who were holding him down and were full of fear. "Please do not touch him. Please sit down and pray. Let me do this."

Then I had to address the demons, and there were many. "Stop manifesting and talk to me!" I commanded. I wanted to be able to talk to this young man without interference from the demons.

"Do you have bitterness in your heart toward anyone?" I asked the young man, still reeling from what was happening around him.

"Yes," he replied. I could see such sadness in his eyes. "My father." Years of physical abuse, neglect, and drunken rages by his father left him open to the spiritual world.

"You have to forgive him." At this point the young pastor was happy to comply, but when I laid hands on him again, the demons came back. One by one, demons of lust, violence, and bitterness were cast out. "You have no authority...he has forgiven his father!"

Interestingly, when all of the demons had left and I spoke to him, he had no awareness of what had just happened or that he was even possessed. He knew he battled lust, anger, and bitterness, but always thought it was simply in his flesh. Now this young leader was free. But like all people who escape the grip of the enemy, they must be surrounded and loved by mature believers who will walk with them.

The above story is shared to make two points. First, to live the Kingdom life in the shadow of his coming, courage is often expressed in facing your own demons, whether they are actual spirits or hidden fears and hurts. Like the young pastor, you will be tempted to get in and out of line for prayer. You have the power of choice to submit yourself to a deep cleansing from the Holy Spirit or not.

It takes great courage – courage needed in these last days to be a person who fears God more than fears man. Possibly, in reading this, you think your "issues" are nowhere near what the young man experienced. Maybe so, however,

> *"You have the power of choice to submit yourself to a deep cleansing from the Holy Spirit or not.*

the more sensitive to the Spirit you become, the more profoundly aware you are of your sin. That awareness should drive you continually to your knees and to the foot of the cross where the joy of forgiveness can be found.

Courage to Go

Second, the Kingdom of God needs courageous warriors, unafraid of Kingdom battles.

"For we wrestle not against flesh and blood, but against principalities, against powers, against the rulers of the darkness of this world, against spiritual wickedness in high places."
Ephesians 6:12 (KJV)

I meet leaders from around the world, true godly warriors, who battle not only in the spirit world, but also in life and death struggles daily. They defy the laws of man to obey the Law of Christ, and do so knowing they may die.

In Sri Lanka, I've watched dozens of young men and women knowingly walk into villages where if the people learned they were Christians, they would beat them to death. And some did die and many more were beaten within an inch of their life.

Did they lack faith? No, they have courage – courage that comes from knowing that Jesus is coming back; courage that comes from knowing this world is but a temporary place because our real home is in heaven; courage that gives you faith to go where no believer has gone; courage to fight the enemy on his turf, to go into the dark places, the godless regions and plant the flag of the gospel; courage to hate evil and fight sin.

So you want the anointing of God?

Do you have the courage from the Lord to go wherever he may send you? And that may not be deep, dark Africa[4], but across the street to your cranky neighbor.

Kingdom Key #21

The anointing will give you great courage to establish the Kingdom of God in the strongholds of the enemy.

For though we walk in the flesh, we do not war according to the flesh. For the weapons of our warfare are not carnal but mighty in God for pulling down strongholds.
2 Corinthians 10:3-4 (NKJV)

Courage to Confront

I have a holy hatred for those who entrap young, innocent victims into the horrors of sex trafficking. If you've traveled as much as I have, you've seen too much for it not to break your heart. Most of the time, there's nothing you can do, but sometimes the opportunity knocks.

I was asked to speak in a region of Sri Lanka known for its prostitution. Many of these young girls came to listen because they had heard about me as someone who "healed." They almost all experienced various ailments and horrible dreams. How they became ensnared in sex trafficking was especially hideous. A local witch doctor would cast spells on them, using demons to possess them – his purpose only to use them.

After sharing the gospel, I prayed for the women, casting out many demons. One by one, they were set free and healed of their ailments. Watching their faces turn from fear to joy and freedom is something I can never forget. Truly I had the privilege of seeing Jesus "setting the captives free."

All of the "Good News" made for one very angry witch doctor that didn't like seeing his business ruined. He must have wanted to make it a very public confrontation, because I saw him standing in the corner of the home where I was speaking.

The witch doctor wasn't merely listening; he was silently casting spells – spells trying to silence me. How did I know? Partly because I could see his lips moving, but largely because I could sense the demonic activity changing the atmosphere of the room. I couldn't ignore him any longer.

> *The witch doctor wasn't merely listening; he was silently casting spells.*

So I challenged him. If this were the old American West, I suppose we would have stepped outside and drawn our pistols. But this fight would involve a power beyond the physical. I stopped my sermon and pointed at him. "I know who you are. I know what you're trying to do. I have the power of God and you'll face the consequences."

I then demanded he come forward.

People often ask, how do you "feel" in such a circumstance? Usually after the initial surge of emotion, a calm peace comes over me. I'm not sure how calm I was in this moment.

As he came close to me, I put out my hand and in Jesus' name rebuked the powers of the demons inside him. He instantly shot back, crashing into a wall and falling flat on his face. He began to scream loud curses at me.

Now I was calm and even felt some pity. Walking over to him, I looked down and asked him, "Would you like to receive Jesus and be free of demonic power?"

Embarrassed, his answer was a terse, "No, leave me alone!" He began to beg for mercy because he couldn't move.

Finally, I forgave him and released him, but demanded he never do the things he had done in this community ever again. Terrified, he ran away, never returning. Seeing his departure, many in the village shared how he had terrorized not just the poor girls, but an entire village.

"The church's mission is to be the presence of the kingdom…The church's mission is to show the world what it looks like when a community of people live under the reign of God."[5]

In this village, the presence of the Kingdom dispelled the presence of darkness. Many were saved, many healed, many set free from being oppressed. As his reign draws near, we must have great courage to take back territory from evil.

This kind of mission requires courage in the Spirit, but it also invokes character.

Character

In these last days, the character of believers is being tested. And I believe we haven't come close to seeing the full fury of hell unleashed yet.

Character, best described in Galatians 5:22-23 by the Fruit of the Spirit, is as critical, if not more, than operating in the Gifts of the Spirit. Of course, it is critical to operate in both simultaneously.

Character is the outgrowth of faithful, fearless walking with our Lord. You cannot have it bestowed on you at a miracle conference; you must daily develop it by living according to the Scriptures and listening to his voice.

Character is forged in the fires of life.

"so that the tested genuineness of your faith—more precious than gold that perishes though it is tested by fire—may be found to result in praise and glory and honor at the revelation of Jesus Christ." 1 Peter 1:7 (ESV)

"Behold, I have refined you, but not as silver; I have tried you in the furnace of affliction." Isaiah 48:10 (ESV)

> "*Character is the outgrowth of faithful, fearless walking with our Lord.*

Kingdom Key #22

The character of the believer is essential in moving in the fruitful anointing of God. How can you bear much fruit in your ministry when you bear little fruit in your life?

By this My Father is glorified, that you bear much fruit; so you will be My disciples.
John 15:8 (NKJV)

Character is also forged in prayer.

"PRAYER governs conduct, and conduct makes character. Conduct is what we do; character is what we are. Conduct is the outward life. Character is the life unseen, hidden within,

yet evidenced by that which is seen…Character is the root of the tree, conduct, the fruit it bears."[6]

Pastor E.M. Bounds continues to link prayer and character…

"The more we pray, the better we are, the purer and better our lives."[7]

The great Puritan preacher and writer John Bunyan famously stated:

"…prayer is a shield to the soul, a sacrifice to God, and a scourge for Satan."[8]

I hesitate to write much on prayer as there are numerous, excellent works on the subject. However, my emphasis here is to link our character to our prayer life. And the two inextricably bound are, and will be, essential in how we operate as anointed vessels in these last days.

The foundation of all God's blessing and moving in Sri Lanka has been, and continues to be, based in prayer. And it has been the fervent prayer of the saints that has developed the character of heart to overcome persecution we have faced.

Prayer, like character, isn't an instant achievement. It stands in contrast to a culture increasingly obstinate to patience and long-suffering. Like it or not, a younger generation lives in a world of sound bites and instant gratification.

In a "Twitter Universe," we of an older era must model to our future leaders not increasingly old prayer paradigms, but rather the essence of relationship that can only be achieved in prayer. And, of course, it is only in that relationship where character is found and nurtured.

I admire the life and writing of Indian missionary Sadhu Sundar Singh who after persecuting believers and becoming suicidal cried out to whatever God (Hindu, Sikh, or Christian) would reveal himself. A vision of Jesus and a life committed to prayer and evangelism led him to write such profound insights into the true purpose of prayer:

> *"Prayer does not mean asking God for all kinds of things we want, it is rather the desire for God Himself.*

"The essence of prayer does not consist in asking God for something but in opening our hearts to God, in speaking with Him, and living with Him in perpetual communion. Prayer is continual abandonment to God. Prayer does not mean asking God for all kinds of things we want, it is rather the desire for God Himself, the only Giver of Life."[9]

I believe it is the obligation, better the privilege, of my generation to live out with our lives this essence of prayer to the next generation. There is a great possibility that they will be the last generation, and if so, they will be tested to "the root of the tree."

Commitment

The Kingdom of God demands people of great courage, character, and of course commitment to the cause.

Commitment in the Kingdom demands focus and a God-given strategy. It must not be beholden to feelings and emotions. Commitment is the engine that keeps our mission moving forward.

Only three years into a credentialed ministry of the Foursquare Church, I was asked to lead its national work in Sri Lanka. All totaled, we had only three house churches and 60 people. Nothing about this appointment excited me. Filled with fear and doubt, my prayers were more like complaints to God.

I compared our little Foursquare movement in Sri Lanka to other denominations and ministries. I compared myself to other leaders of these ministries. Have you ever felt like a failure when you measured yourself to other more "successful" peers? I sure did.

Comparison grew to envy. Envy blossomed into full-blown jealousy. Heard of the Positive Confession movement? Well, I could have founded the Church of the Negative Word. I even considered going full-time into my trained profession, accounting, and giving up the ministry.

In the midst of this avalanche of self-pity, I heard the voice of the Lord, "Do your best with what little you have."

My response? "We have nothing, Lord."

But the gentle reminder from God came to me. I had my wonderful family, three faithful pastors, and a group of believers. God had given me five loaves and two fish; and I only needed to trust him for the rest.

The "Sri Lankan Miracle" became a series of situations where we had to trust the Lord for provision, for power, and for protection, offering our lives filled with passion, purpose, and of course, prayer to the Lord.

Provision

I've written much on the power and protection of God. Yet, one of the equally miraculous signs of the Lord is his provision.

In these last days, we must be open to supernatural ways in which the Father takes care of his children's needs.

I've heard the saying, "Where God guides, he provides,"[10] and couldn't agree more. Thousands of times, both as an individual family and a nationwide church family, we've seen the Lord manifest himself with the perfect provision. Of course, the key is operating in his guidance. We shouldn't expect provision to follow our flesh.

The Lord is looking for those he can trust with finances. In the Kingdom of God there is no lack of provision – only lack of trust. Can we be trusted with all that God desires to bless us with? Part of the answer is how we respond to the question. Do we primarily view the financial and material blessings of God in terms of personal gain or Kingdom advancement? Let's be honest, far too many leaders have confused the two. Even in Paul's day, preachers failed this temptation.

"For we are not, as so many, peddling the word of God."
2 Corinthians 2:17 (NKJV)

As someone who literally travels the world, I have seen far too often pastors gain extraordinary personal wealth even while those in their congregations suffer in poverty. This must break the Lord's heart.

Just as there is a grave misunderstanding of God's prosperity to his people, there too is sad timidity in trusting him for financial blessing. It takes faith to step out into situations God has called you to that require provision you do not have. Again, the qualifier is God's guiding. And I may add, we can never use laziness or lack of preparation as an excuse to call on God in desperation.

Yet again, I must ask, "Are we trusting God?" Are we trusting him with our personal financial situation? Are we trusting him with our ministry to provide beyond the natural? In these last days, I believe many will be called to step out in faith, not for personal gain, but to see the Kingdom of God move forward.

The Desperate Deadline

I was shocked. Standing at the door of our humble home in the slums of Colombo stood the towering figure of Dr. Paul Risser and his wife, Marilee. Dr. Risser, one of the most respected leaders

> *In these last days, I believe many will be called to step out in faith, not for personal gain, but to see the Kingdom of God move forward.*

in our Foursquare movement, greeted me in his warm Texas twang, "Well, hello Leslie!"

It took me a moment to compose myself and invite them in. Their story, as well as ours, would eventually play out like an impossible plotline from a made-for-TV movie.

After nearly five years of pioneering work, Belen and I were sensing in our spirits that it was time to move our church from the slums into the suburbs of Colombo. Part of the challenge we faced was the need to purchase property and a building to call our headquarters – a government requirement.

When we found the perfect property and facility we negotiated a price of $67,000, provided that it be paid in full by the end of the month. The only problem – we had $10 to our name and the church less. But I had made a promise to the landowner and believed God would provide.

Some may call our step of faith foolishness or presumption. All I knew at the moment, I had to fast. By the fourth day, a strong sense that the Lord had answered our prayers overcame me; therefore, I broke the fast. It occurred just in time to cast out multiple demons in a poor young girl found running through the streets, causing chaos in the community. I had no idea the Rissers were on their way to our house and it took the very guidance of

God to get them there.

A supernatural sense overwhelmed Dr. Risser to see me. Though he did not have our address, out of sheer obedience he willingly boarded a plane for Sri Lanka. Upon arrival at the airport, he asked numerous taxi drivers if they knew who I was. Of course, because the Lord was in full control, one of the taxi drivers knew me and where I lived. Paul, wife Marilee, and two other women from Florence Avenue Foursquare Church were driven directly to our home, the only identification marker a tree, no street number.

After my shaky welcome, I asked them why they had come so far to honor us. Their response: simply to see our ministry and determine our needs. When they asked to see our church building, I told them the story of purchasing the property. They insisted on seeing it immediately. Once there, I began to prayer walk and Paul spoke to the landowner. I confess to being more than a little intimidated when telling Paul the whole story. But I knew they were our answer to much prayer and fasting.

On the very day the $67,000 came due it arrived in our bank, thanks to the incredible obedience of the Rissers. I learned much from the experience: first, to be wise in negotiations, but most importantly, to never stop trusting the Lord for provision.

Kingdom Key #23

When God's anointing comes to advance the Kingdom of God, trust for his provision where it is needed, from whomever he has called.

Let them do good, that they be rich in good works, ready to give, willing to share, storing up for themselves a good foundation for the time to come, that they may lay hold on eternal life.
1 Timothy 6:18-19 (NKJV)

More Dreams

God speaks often to me through dreams. Often those dreams are about Jesus' coming. I look forward to them as I always awake refreshed and full of joy and strength.

Often the dreams involve the Lord instructing me about walking away from sin, failure, or depression and climbing into his loving arms. I wake up from these dreams recommitted to share his love with others.

Only a few years ago, a dream left a profound impact on me and our churches. In this dream, I saw myself sitting opposite someone I've never met before. I began a conversation with this stranger I believed an angel and heard him say, "Share what is in you heart…what do you see?"

As soon as the words were spoken, spectacular things began to take place before my eyes.

Multitudes of people, joined by angels, together lifting up their hands with songs of praise, like the sound of many waters, changing the entire atmosphere. The sound was soothing, refreshing, freeing all from any anxiety or stress. The place filled with a cloud of glory, lifting up the praise to the Most Holy Place.

We continued to worship the Lord God Almighty and people were healed, set free, only joy and complete freedom filled our hearts. In the midst of this, the Lord gave me a word of prophecy:

> *"The place filled with a cloud of glory, lifting up the praise to the Most Holy Place.*

God is about to pour out his spirit in an unprecedented manner on our land and on the nations. The Spirit of the Lord will flow like a river from the north of Sri Lanka and it will flood the entire nation.

The outpouring of the Holy Spirit will result in ethnic reconciliation, national reformation, restoration, and transformation affecting every sphere of life. God is about to release a great blessing on our nation that will break the curse of hatred, bloodguilt, and shedding of innocent blood. The River of God will flow like a raging fire, burning up the dross of shame and the filth of sin in the cities, villages, streets, and every nook and cranny of our beloved nation.

As the river of God's fire begins to blaze through our communities, burning up the dross, it will light the places of gross darkness, dispelling all fear, anguish, and hopelessness. The fire of God will embrace the entire nation, pulling down satanic principality strongholds and casting out ruling spirits of seduction, sadism, and all forms of wickedness, witchcraft, idolatry, and immorality.

Out of the raging fire of God sparks will fly out reaching the nations, precisely targeting where the Sri Lankan diaspora has spread. Reconciliation, healing, transformation, and miracles will begin to take place among them as well. Our God-led efforts in sending missionaries to nations our fellow Sri Lankans have migrated to will be greatly rewarded by many thousands coming to the Lord and being reconciled to one another across ethnic lines.

I believe that we are on the verge of a mighty move of God before he brings into his barn his end time harvest. Therefore, may we with great hope and anticipation prepare ourselves for this unprecedented move of God which is going to bring the nations and all peoples on earth, both great and small, on their knees before the King of Kings and Lord of Lords. Jesus is getting ready to return for us, his beautiful bride. May we therefore remember it is not about you or me, it is about Jesus.

May we serve him with a deeper devotion, live for him with a more focused vision, and give for his Kingdom's cause with a generosity which is unparalleled by the world.

Amen.

> *"May we therefore remember it is not about you or me, it is about Jesus.*

I pray this word inspires you and challenges you to be a part, wherever you may live, of his end time army. Whether you believe you are a general or a private, the battle rages on with or without you. But better with you…much better.

Kingdom Key #24

The anointing of God comes both with a purpose and a price. It is not bestowed lightly or for individual glory. It comes only to bring him glory and to bring heaven to earth.

Our Father which art in heaven,

hallowed be thy name. Thy kingdom come,

thy will be done in earth, as it is in heaven …

Matthew 6:9-10 (KJV)

May the Spirit of our Lord anoint you to preach the gospel, to live the gospel, to be the gospel until he comes.

*D*ear Lord, we thank you very much for bringing us into the hope of eternal life. We are now able to live in anticipation of your imminent return. The signs of the times show us very clearly that you are about to return to take us, your bride, to your home.

*Dear Lord, your word in 1 John 3:3 says, "**Everyone who has this hope in Him purifies himself, just as He is pure.**" I pray that you would give each of us the grace to watch for your coming and to* *walk in purity. I pray you would be released from the strangle hold of sin and be filled in the power of God's Holy Spirit and prepare yourself for the coming of our Lord. In Jesus' name, amen.*

8

FINAL WORDS ON THE ANOINTING

"My food is to do the will of Him who sent Me, and to finish His work." John 4:34 (NIV)

"Most assuredly, I say to you, the Son can do nothing of Himself but what He sees the Father do; for whatever He does, the son also does in like manner." John 5:19 (NKJV)

It is indeed humbling to realize that Jesus depended on the anointing to achieve the purposes of his father. To state it bluntly, if Jesus needed the anointing, how can any disciple not seek it in its fullness? After all, the word *Christ* means Anointed One.

The Anointing is Someone

While all believers are indwelled by the Holy Spirit (see Romans 8), the obvious truth is some walk more closely in the Spirit. The anointing is an impartation of someone, not something, that brings glory to God. It is not a flow of some supernatural energy or power; it is a person, the Holy Spirit, in our lives.

Pastor Bill Johnson states it succinctly:

"This anointing is actually the person of the Holy Spirit upon someone to equip them for supernatural endeavors."[1]

Therefore, the anointing is a lifestyle of intimate relationship with the Holy Spirit as Jesus perfectly modeled. The Apostle Paul helps us understand the deep relational aspect of the Third Person's work in our lives in Romans 8:15-16.

"For you did not receive the spirit of bondage again to fear, but you received the Spirit of adoption by whom we cry out, 'Abba, Father.' The Spirit Himself bears witness with our spirit that we are children of God." (NKJV)

The anointing flows out of relationship that is refined through a lifestyle. Too many believers see the acquisition of the anointing as if they are Clark Kent just before entering the phone booth and emerging as Superman. One doesn't request the anointing for a momentary supernatural manifestation; it flows from a set apart life. The anointing, as described in the Old Testament, especially in Exodus 40, was a lifetime commitment to a lifestyle of consecration to God.

"…For their anointing shall surely be an everlasting priesthood throughout their generations." Exodus 40:15 (NKJV)

Of course, because of Jesus' ultimate sacrifice, we all have the opportunity to become a part of a royal priesthood (1 Peter 2:9) with all the privileges that entails, including the anointing, should we choose to walk in it.

The Anointing as a Lifestyle

As stated before, too many believers view the anointing almost in terms of a performance, especially connected to ministry. "That preacher was anointed" or "that man has the anointing to heal" are common expressions after a service. If there is a real anointing, it flows from a deep understanding of the Holy Spirit based in a lifestyle committed to

> *If there is a real anointing, it flows from a deep understanding of the Holy Spirit based in a lifestyle committed to the Triune God.*

the Triune God. It's simply living each day willing to hear "what the Spirit is saying" and then acting upon what he says. The more you live this out, the more your ability to hear clearly becomes. The supernatural becomes, if you will, a part of your natural existence. Spending hours in prayer becomes less and less an ecclesiastical requirement and more a tender encounter.

I share this only to illustrate the point, but I daily spend hours in prayer, often as Paul described as "unceasing prayer." My life is a day-to-day, hour-by-hour communion with God. This is why I emphasize speaking in tongues, so that your spirit can communicate directly with the Holy Spirit. I've found it essential to an ongoing intimate communion; and it's something I learned in my youth.

My grandmother, although uneducated, moved in the anointing of God as powerfully as anyone I've ever met. More than anyone else in my large family, I was preoccupied in learning what gave her such power. I would often sit by her closed door to listen to her prayers. Every morning before school I went to her to get prayer and an anointing of oil.

That's why I love the second letters of Paul to Timothy, especially verses 5 and 6 of chapter one.

"When I call to remembrance the genuine faith that is in you,
which dwelt first in your grandmother Lois…Therefore I remind you
to stir up the gift of God which is in you through the laying on of my
hands." (NKJV)

Kingdom Key #25

Moving in the anointing flows from a lifestyle of
intimate relationship with the Holy Spirit.

For in him dwells all the fullness of the Godhead
bodily; and you are complete in Him.
Colossians 2:9-10 (NKJV)

The Gifts and Fruit of the Anointing

Being in such an ongoing relationship will produce fruit
and expressions of grace. The grace gifts or *Charismata* as

described in 1 Corinthians 12 are a manifestation of the Spirit given for the benefit of all.

Simply stated, the anointing will often be realized through a gift of the Spirit whether it is tongues, healing, prophecy, or some miracle. Of course, there are many books written to further describe each gift of the Spirit. But for the believer to actively move in the anointing and not be open to using the gifts would be like a baker unwilling to use flour, butter, or yeast in their bread.

Chapter 12 of 1 Corinthians is purposefully linked to chapter 13 and the supremacy of love. This leads to the Fruit of the Spirit being, as with the Gifts, essential to the manifestation of the anointing of God.

Paul, in his quest of a deeper walk with his Lord, described it in terms of an ongoing, growing process culminated in the coming of the Lord.

"For now we see in a mirror, dimly, but then face to face. Now I know in part, but then I shall know just as I also am known. And now abide faith, hope, love, these three, but the greatest of these is love." 1 Corinthians 13:12-13 (NKJV)

Paul, in Galatians 5, contrasts the words of the flesh with those of the Spirit, which he lists in verses 22 and 23. He summarizes with the foundational statement in verse 25.

"If we live in the Spirit, let us also walk in the Spirit." (KJV)

If we as believers are indwelled by the Holy Spirit, then there will be a pouring out of the Holy Spirit in our daily lives.

Love, joy, peace, longsuffering, kindness, goodness, faithfulness, gentleness, and self-control will be powerful manifestations of the presence of God – especially when they are juxtaposed in a situation when the flesh would normally dominate.

An even more powerful example of God's anointing occurs when both the gifts and fruit are operating simultaneously, all for the benefit of his children.

Armenia

Visiting Armenia, in the roar of winter, especially for a Sri Lankan is not wise. Yet, when the Lord calls, the servant follows.

> *If we as believers are indwelled by the Holy Spirit, then there will be a pouring out of the Holy Spirit in our daily lives.*

When the servant follows, the Holy Spirit comes too; and nothing can be more joyful, even in sub-freezing temperatures.

In only five days, over 5,000 people gave their hearts to Christ. More were healed than usual, including multiple deaf and blind people.

They brought an emaciated young man on a makeshift stretcher to the stage of the church. As he lay there looking up at me, I could not fully comprehend dying of cancer while being homeless and alone.

After preaching the gospel, I prayed and asked the Lord to pour out his Spirit upon all who were sick and afflicted. I did not lay hands on anyone individually.

Almost instantly after my prayer, this young man stood up and began jumping up and down, grabbing my microphone to proclaim his healing. His once near lifeless body radiant with energy and free of cancer. I found myself both moved with compassion and empowered by the presence of God, not only for this young man, but also from the hundreds of faces reflecting their quiet desperation.

The next day after preaching, a long line developed. A ten-year-old girl with beautiful coal black hair, who reminded me of my own daughter, needed healing from total deafness. I prayed for her, but nothing happened. She got in the line again. I prayed again. Nothing happened. By her fourth time around I cried out to God, "Lord, I am desperate. You must touch this girl. She cannot go home without being healed."

When the gifts and the fruit of the Spirit come together, it is a wonderful thing. You feel the surge of compassion and the joy of expectancy. You know at that moment you are a pure conduit of his love.

She fell under the weight of that love and got up proclaiming, "I'm healed! I'm healed!"

When she came through the prayer line a fifth time I looked at her perplexed. Did the healing leave? What was happening?

"I want to be able to sing on the worship team. I want to have an ear for music."

I prayed again, this time smiling and believing she would soon give the angels at the throne of heaven competition with her beautiful song.

The Anointing as Good News and Warfare

The anointing involves not only manifestations of the gifts and fruit of the Spirit, but also a proclamation of the core of the gospel message:

- The good news that a resurrected Jesus can create in us a clean heart, spotless and perfect before the Father
- Setting captives free with a message of hope and grace that can drive out the deepest depression or addiction
- Proclaiming the favorable year of the Lord, a message of God's grace and mercy to those ignorant of it

The anointing will break the yoke.

"…the yoke shall be destroyed because of the anointing."
Isaiah 10:27 (KJV)

Good News

Preaching the gospel, whether to thousands in a stadium or across the table at a Starbucks, is always more effective under the anointing of the Holy Spirit.

Unfortunately, personal evangelism can be perceived as the mere sharing of facts. But the anointing is critical to not only clearly share the gospel, but also for the hearer to understand and receive truth from the Holy Spirit.

Jesus, of course, understood this, often repeating a refrain as he did after sharing the Parable of the Sower.

"He who has ears to hear, let him hear!" Luke 8:8 (NKJV)

Someone who desires to move in the anointing should always be open to hearing what the Spirit is saying regarding someone's spiritual status. I believe too many who come to our churches may never have received Christ; and they become involved for years, yet never fully grasp the great truth of the Good News. We need believers who are sensitive to the Spirit to discern those who are truly saved from those who are not.

Possibly one of the greatest mission fields exists inside our churches!

This sad truth never seemed more evident than when I traveled to Bangladesh to meet leaders wishing to join the Foursquare Church movement.

On my way to Khulna, Bangladesh I began to review my Foursquare polity, preparing to inform leaders, most I understood to be pastors, some of the key aspects of

> **"Possibly one of the greatest mission fields exists inside our churches!**

joining our movement. Yet, as I looked over notes and tried to make preparations, the Holy Spirit had other plans for me.

I could only seem to focus on a simple gospel message and to prepare myself spiritually to minister the Baptism of the Holy Spirit. Once I arrived and continued studying, the voice inside me became clearer. "You are preparing to teach Foursquare doctrine and polity. What if they need to hear the simple gospel message?"

I knew I must yield to the Holy Spirit and shared the gospel with all 25 leaders. I even recited a Sinner's Prayer. I asked, "How many of you have not prayed a prayer like this before?" They all raised their hands.

I thought possibly I needed to rephrase the question. "How many among you have ever prayed this prayer before?" No one raised their hand.

Leading them in the Sinner's Prayer, everyone received Jesus, for the first time, into their lives. Immediately, I taught them about water baptism and proceeded to baptize them all. Right after their water baptisms, I preached about the baptism in the Holy Spirit. Many were filled; some experienced demonic deliverance and also were filled with the Holy Spirit.

Others were healed physically. In a real way, the Foursquare Church in Bangladesh was born.

Warfare

People today are under such bondage, oppression, that it takes an anointing from God to lift that yoke from around their necks. It often reaches a point beyond socio-economic deprivation – a spiritual, demonic oppression.

This is where there must be a spiritual dimension to any humanitarian effort. Anyone who wishes to be the hands of Christ by serving the hungry, the prisoner, the poor must be equipped to see beyond the obvious need and into the spiritual dimension. Sometimes those dimensions include entire cultural oppressions that come as a result of years of spiritual bondage.

In Sri Lanka, entire villages have fallen under a spiritual oppression, sometimes due to years of fallen cultures and sometimes due to an assigned demonic entity. This type of yoke must be broken and the anointing will give understanding and Spirit-led directives.

Don't be naïve to think such bondages apply only to backward villages. I believe there are major cities in first world nations living under both the bondage of corrupt culture and the assignment of an evil principality.

The anointed of God are called to break such strongholds. Such strongholds are religious spirits and post modernism. They are counterfeits of the Holy Spirit, fighting revival so needed in the Western world. These spirits move subtly. They fight any attempt to experience the current presence of God, preferring that the Christian's walk be moored in only doctrine and in the past. Any attempt to be led by the Spirit and move in the anointing is viewed as suspect and full of the possibility of deception.

A person moving under the unction of the Holy Spirit moves with a faith rooted in the Word, both as a hearer (a student) and a doer also. In fact, part of the anointing of God empowers us to know God's truth as opposed to error (1 John 2:20, 26, 27).

"For though we walk in the flesh, we do not war according to the flesh. For the weapons of our warfare are not carnal but mighty in God for pulling down strongholds."

2 Corinthians 10:3-4 (NKJV)

> **A person moving under the unction of the Holy Spirit moves with a faith rooted in the Word.**

The Emotional Part of the Anointing

We are created to experience life, including God, with emotion. Despite what some believers may think, God wants us to know him both through our mind and our soul (Luke 10:27). He also wants us to express him to others through our emotion, not just declarations of faith.

Unfortunately, so many, even in the Body of Christ, live with damaged emotions and therefore their emotional expressions are negatively affected. This has caused fear and a desire to remain as emotionally free as possible when ministering the gospel.

I have found that moving in the anointing is an emotional experience. Yet, in stating that, the emotion may not be what you might think. Often times, I'm overcome with a powerful tranquil peace before, during, and after a time of ministry. In the Vineyard Churches, and specifically John Wimber's, they described this state as "dialing down" in stark contrast to the more flamboyant healing evangelists as seen on TV.

Once, in Sri Lanka, when walking from my car to the meeting place, people had lined up outside to greet me. Many were sick and diseased. I could feel the anointing being released and saw it as people fell down in rows under its power. They were not "trained" or conditioned to do so.

I've been filled with excitement, anticipation, and with an overwhelming sense of joy. There have been times I felt absolutely nothing, yet saw God move powerfully.

I love the times of raw, pure emotion, but never depend upon them for his anointing. What I depend completely on, especially before any meeting, is getting in the presence of God. Usually this means getting alone two to three hours before any event. I endeavor in this time to empty myself, giving all fears and doubts to him and allowing him to fill all the empty spaces. Though I am an imperfect vessel, my heart's desire is to see his glory made manifest in the lives of the lost, broken, and hurting.

Possibly, my experience is a part of what Paul is referring to in Philippians 2:17.

"Yes, and if I am being poured out as a drink offering on the sacrifice and service of your faith, I am glad and rejoice with you all." (NKJV)

Moving in the anointing involves managing your emotions. Getting "worked up" for theatrical effect is just the flesh and will reap the flesh. Being fearful when looking out at a large crowd or when being confronted by a particularly vocal demon can also affect the flow of God. Fear and faith don't work well together.

What always assists in centering my emotions and allowing me to not be distracted so I can better hear the Spirit, is recalling the heart of Jesus. It was, is, and will be his mission to allow the Spirit of the Lord to anoint him to preach the gospel to the poor, proclaim the release to the captives, set free the oppressed, and see the recovery to the blind.

Aligning my heart with his mission gives me the ultimate emotional stability. It transcends any momentary emotional fluctuation. It centers my mind, heart, and soul on his great love for us. After all, perfect love drives out fear.[2]

No matter what emotion, it is in the anointing, in the realm of the Spirit, where we all should long to be. When we are there, it should feel like home, yet, even better than home; it should be a place we never want to leave.

> *"Aligning my heart with his mission gives me the ultimate emotional stability.*

My Final Prayer of Impartation for You

*D*ear Lord Jesus, I thank you for this dear one who has read this book carefully and has been deeply touched by your Spirit. Thank you, Lord, for working deeply in their heart and for creating in them a desire to be filled, walk, and minister in the fullness of your Spirit.

Dear Lord, now as they draw close to you in prayer for an overflowing, Spirit-filled and Spirit-empowered life, I pray that you would anoint them this very moment.

By God's grace imparted to me, I impart to you the fullness of the Spirit to live and function in the powerful anointing of God. I release God's anointing upon your life that you might be empowered powerfully to move in miracles, signs, wonders, and healings. I bless you to be filled with power to live a godly life manifesting all the fruit of the Spirit. I free you to function in the Holy Spirit's authority that demons would flee as you minister to the spiritually bound.

I free you in the power of the Holy Spirit to be the person God wills you to be. In Jesus' holy and powerful name I pray, AMEN.

9

AFTERWORD: GO IN GRACE

The dull clang of the cell doors closing.

Nothing like sitting in jail – a foreign jail – to increase your prayer life. Across from me a cellmate with a face much too hard for his young age, his eyes fixed on the cracks in the concrete floor. I didn't sense any room for small talk, but the fact that he was Sri Lankan would make an introduction more probable.

Just the day before, I ministered in Thailand and a few days before that in Kuala Lumpur, Malaysia. I saw God's great love for his people expressed through his word and confirmed with power. Hong Kong would be my final stop for their Foursquare

National Convention. At least I thought it would be…
immigration authorities had other ideas.

A two-hour interview that grew into a full interrogation
began to cause me concern. But years of travel into countries
much more authoritarian taught me a certain set of diplomatic
skills. You may be very afraid, but it's best to keep emotions to
yourself. It didn't seem to matter that all my papers were in
order; however, I made sure all my prayers were also in order.
The interrogation went on throughout the night, every hour on
the hour. No food, water, or sleep, just the cold bench of a jail
cell and the weight of the unknown. Between the intense
encounters with the authorities, I started a conversation with
my young cellmate. I began by talking about Jesus.

It no doubt was the last thing he wanted to hear. Angry,
scared, he knew he would be deported back to Sri Lanka. Since
he was a member of a terrorist organization, the possibility of a
life sentence loomed large.

It didn't take long for him to lower his guard and open up
to me. Neither of us expected to sleep. The sounds of jail, even
late into the night, could wake the dead.

The concept of grace is not an easy thing to be grasped by
Buddhists, Hindus, or Muslims. The very idea of a divine gift,

given without condition and involving salvation, runs contrary to all their background and teaching. The core of each faith is centered around what one must do rather than what God is doing. Each of these religions involves a type of fatalism where the devotee does all they can do, but in the end it is left up to fate. The intensely personal exchange with the Almighty via grace takes a true Spirit-led opening of the heart.[1]

I shared with this young man about this grace that could only be extended to him because of Jesus' sacrifice. I told him how God was a god of second chances and his grace was all about forgiveness and mercy.

I never asked the young man to recount his many sins to me. No doubt his past life was filled with death and destruction. I felt like I could see his past lift from his shoulders as he began to give his troubled heart to Christ, those sullen eyes now filled with tears of joy. I asked him to pray with me the Sinner's Prayer. In that dark, cold cell, a blanket of warmth covered us both. The presence of Jesus filled the room and filled our hearts.

In that divine moment, someone deserving of judgment received the ultimate pardon. Yes, the world may still exact punishment for his earthly crimes, but in that jail cell the God of the universe came in mercy and love. Grace is God's gift to us and yet, somehow, maybe because of fear, maybe misunderstanding, we too often fail to pass it on to others.

A Sad Truth

My encounter with grace in a Hong Kong jail cell is a metaphor of the Church today. As believers, we come across people, everyday, who are imprisoned within their own lives. No ethnic, social, economic, or religious exceptions – spiritual bankruptcy is rampant and growing.

Yet, we hide that most beautifully wrapped divine gift from almost everyone we meet – a gift that will free them from their personal prison. Why? What are we afraid of? The statistics of believers who have never shared the gospel to someone outside their family is staggeringly sad.

Maybe it's because we haven't fully experienced grace. We haven't allowed it to find the deepest places in our hearts and minds. Author Philip Yancey has said:

"Grace, like water, flows to the lowest part, to those who admit a need and welcome the news that God loves even them."[2]

We must live and breathe grace.

Grace isn't an existential state of mind, but a way of life. It doesn't take a theologian to spot a person who lives in grace – because they extend it to others. A great practitioner of our faith, Rick Warren, once wrote:

"When you've experienced grace and you feel like you've been forgiven, you're a lot more forgiving of other people. You're a lot more gracious to others."[3]

And when you live that way, inevitably others notice and will want to know why. Sharing will be a natural outflow of your living out these two great commandments: loving God and loving your neighbor as yourself.

So What's the Problem?

I believe the Lord is raising up an army of believers – men, women, young, and old. They will be anointed for battle. They will plant the flag of the Kingdom of God in territory the enemy has occupied.

This army is well equipped in the Word of God and will walk in it, full of faith, as never before. The culture will try to shame them into submission. The enemy will try to turn their faith into fear.

> *We must live and breathe grace.*

Even the "church" will doubt and question, wanting to debate rather than do.

Theological and doctrinal issues will be used to slow this army down, but this force receives their "marching orders" from the Holy Spirit. These generals in the Spirit will know and trust their field commanders who, in turn, will follow orders and lead by example – and the faithful soldiers will follow.

They will march into the halls of power, entertainment, and science. The arts from these anointed will reflect a creative edge that only God can breathe. Science will experience the kind of breakthrough that begs the question, "Were they inspired?" And the powerful will lay down their power to honor God and man. Only those anointed for these battles will make the lasting difference, the eternal mark.

What will allow them access into these places of influence? Each one, even the youngest among them, will be full of grace. The world cannot resist real grace. It is what ultimately gave Mother Teresa access to an audience full of kings and presidents. It filled her eyes and flowed from her lips.

> *"The world cannot resist real grace.*

Grace overcomes our divisions. Yes, even our doctrinal differences. It unites us to move for one purpose: Give grace to another.

> *Grace is, in fact, missional. It transcends culture.*

Grace is, in fact, missional. It transcends culture. The young Hindu boy in the Hong Kong jail joyfully received it despite every cultural and religious objection.

But know this: Grace attracts the sinners. It will bring into our safe houses of worship the same people Jesus attracted to himself. And like the religious leaders during his time, they were none too happy. It will be messy, but Kingdom work is always messy.

This army, however, will not be confined to bringing the lost into the walls of the church. They will build his church wherever it is needed and it will not be built to look like anything we've known before. The sinners will fill it up and the religious self-righteous will be far away.

Mercy will reign. Grace is sufficient. The Kingdom of God will reach into every sector of society. Philip Yancey writes:

Jesus moved the emphasis from God's holiness (exclusive) to God's mercy (inclusive). Instead of the message, "No

undesirables allowed," he proclaimed, "In God's Kingdom there are no undesirables." By going out of his way to meet with Gentiles, eat with sinners and touch the sick, he extended the realm of God's mercy.[4]

What's Left to Do?

Recommit yourself to being a person of grace. Allow it, like the alabaster jar of anointing oil, to flow over you. Give the Holy Spirit access to the deepest places in your heart and mind.

Forgive those who have wounded you. Forgive everyone who has said or done anything to cause you pain. Ask forgiveness of those you have hurt. Be free of the shackles of unforgiveness but do so under the presence and guiding hand of the Holy Spirit. Trust him to show you, to lead you.

Spend time at the foot of the cross – not to wallow in your past sins, but to come grateful, thankful to the one whose death made your new life possible. Let worship come unashamed and unafraid. Don't let the Michal's in your life keep you from dancing and worshiping as David did.

Know grace is real. You are forgiven by God because of what Jesus did. You cannot add one more thing. You cannot do anything more to get more love from God – or more forgiveness or even more grace.

Jesus did it all, all to him we owe.

Flowing from your life, acutely aware of your sin and even more aware of how it's been forgiven, will be the life of grace – extended to others.

Since I've used a metaphor of an army earlier in this chapter, allow me to share from a scene of an epic war movie, *Saving Private Ryan.*[5]

At the end of the movie, based on D-Day in Europe, the company of Army Rangers led by Sgt. Miller (Tom Hanks) finds alive, after much searching, Pvt. James Ryan (Matt Damon). Pvt. Ryan is the remaining son of a mother who has already lost her other three sons to the war. A fierce battle over a bridge kills most of this company and leaves Sgt. Miller mortally wounded. He takes his last breaths to tell Pvt. Ryan, whom he has drawn close to himself to whisper, "Earn this."

The image of Pvt. Ryan morphs into an old man standing some 60 years later at the grave of this brave sergeant. He is joined by his wife while his children and

> *You cannot do anything more to get more love from God.*

195

grandchildren wait in the distance. As if he's speaking to her so that Sgt. Miller could hear it, he says to his wife, "Tell me that I've led a good life."

In this closing scene of a great movie, it's clear that he has, and that in a real way, over the years, he "earned it." Their sacrifice made his "good" life possible.

It's a wonderful visual of the grace of Jesus Christ.

Nothing Private Ryan did saved him; it was the collective effort of courageous men. But now that he was saved from the war, to honor those brave men, he thought about their "sacrifice at the bridge" every day. It was that deep realization of their great sacrifice that guided him to live a good and honorable life. They gave their very lives for him; he could only respond to this act of grace by living a life worthy of their sacrifice.

In a similar way, we who have put our trust in Jesus and the work he did at the cross must be always aware of such loving sacrifice – to remind ourselves every day there is nothing more we can add, our only response is to live to bring him honor and glory. It's in this light where "cheap grace" is exposed and the real grace is lived.

Thomas Merton once said:

"A saint is not someone who is good but someone who experiences the goodness of God."[6]

Grace is extolling his goodness, not explaining how bad we are. Yet people of grace aren't afraid to be themselves, warts and all, because as Brennan Manning states, **"If we trust grace, we don't need to hide who we are from one another."**[7]

Can you imagine this army of grace-filled warriors? Can you consider the power that will come from their weakness? Because when they are weak, he is strong.

"But he said to me, 'My grace is sufficient for you, for my power is made perfect in weakness.' Therefore I will boast all the more gladly about my weaknesses, so that Christ's power may rest on me." 2 Corinthians 12:9 (NIV)

The Lord is desiring people who understand and embrace grace to rest in his anointing. In that holy place, we will receive our orders. Like the first disciples, he will bid you to "come follow me."

He desires you. He desires your presence. The rest of his army awaits you.

NOTES

Introduction

1. John Wimber, Kevin Springer, *Power Evangelism*, page 19 (Chosen Books, 2014)

Chapter 1

1. *The Journal of John Wesley*, entry on January 1, 1739 (Moody Press, 1951)

2. Bill Johnson, *When Heaven Invades Earth*, page 106 (Destiny Image Books, 2013)

3. Medical definition of Approach-Avoidance Conflict: psychological conflict that results when the goal is both desirable and undesirable – *Miriam Webster Medical Dictionary*

4. Philippians 2:5 KJV

5. John Wimber, founder of The Vineyard Church, originated the phrase "Power Encounter" in regard to

the kingdom clash between God and the devil, and is the author of *Power Evangelism* along with Kevin Springer.

6. According to Glenn Stanton from the Gospel Coalition, St. Francis never spoke the phrase "Preach the gospel . . ." Nevertheless, like many famous misapplied or misquoted quotes, it remains in the popular culture.

Chapter 2

1. Spiritual Mapping refers to, according to Cindy Jacobs, the researching of a city to discern any inroads Satan has made, which prevents the spread of the gospel.

2. Belen and I continue to be grateful to God for saving us, but feel deep sorrow over the loss this unfortunate family experienced.

3. Brennan Manning, *All is Grace*, page 192 (David C. Cook, 2011)

4. Mark Batterson, *In a Pit with a Lion on a Snowy Day*, page 22 (Multnomah Books, 2006)

Chapter 3

1. Verse from the song *Hark the Herald Angels Sing* by Charles Wesley

Chapter 4

1. John Wimber, Kevin Springer, *Power Evangelism,* page 178 (Chosen Books, 2014)

2. Leonard Ravenhill, *The Power of His Resurrection* (©Leonard Ravenhill, 1996, Lindale, Texas)

Chapter 5

1. Luke 7:50

2. Robert Linthicum, *Transforming Power,* page 40 (InterVarsity Press, 2003)

3. Robert Linthicum, *City of God, City of Satan,* page 172 (Zondervan Publishing House, 1991)

Chapter 6

1. John 17:16, 2 Corinthians 5:20

Chapter 7

1. The Foursquare Gospel refers to the doctrinal essence of the movement of churches founded by Sister Aimee Semple McPherson in 1923: Jesus the Savior, Jesus the Baptizer, Jesus the Healer, Jesus the Soon Coming King.

2. The J. Herbert Kane quote refers to something I remember reading years ago but could not find the specific reference to.

3. Bishop Robert F. Vasa, from the Nov/Dec 2006 issue of *Lay Witness* magazine (cuf.org)

4. By referring to an early phrase, "deep, dark Africa," I was referencing a missiological stereotype that believers sometimes have toward a call from God. Africa, in fact, has become highly evangelized.

5. Robert Webber, *The Younger Evangelicals: Facing the Challenges of the New World*, page 133 (Baker Books, 2002)

6. E. M. Bounds, *The Necessity of Prayer*, Chapter 8 (holypig.com)

7. E. M. Bounds, *The Necessity of Prayer*, Chapter 8 (holypig.com)

8. John Bunyan, AZQuotes.com, Wind and Fly LTD 2017. http://www.azquotes.com/quote/491595

9. Sadhu Sundar Singh, from the website shalominthewilderness.com (December 8, 2015)

10. "Where God guides, he provides." I am not aware of the original author of this phrase. However, I heard it often around Youth With a Mission participants.

Chapter 8

1. Bill Johnson, *When Heaven Invades Earth,* page 262 (Destiny Image Books, 2013)

2. 1 John 4:18

Chapter 9

1. Suggested reading on the topic of grace; *Embracing Grace* by Daniel A. Brown PhD (Authentic Publishers 2013)

2. Rik Bokelman, May 20, 2016, HelloChristian.com (Excerpt from interview with Philip Yancey)

3. Rick Warren, BrainyQuote.com, Explore Inc. 2017. https://www.brainyquote.com/quotes/quotes/r/rickwarr en394615.html

4. Philip Yancey, *The Jesus I Never Knew*, page 155 (Zondervan, 1995)

5. I realize that even the act of viewing movies is offensive to some. Please accept my sincere apologies if this illustration offends you.

6. Philip Yancey (quoting Thomas Merton), *The Jesus I Never Knew*, page 25 (Zondervan, 1995)

7. Brennan Manning, *All is Grace*, page 20 (David C. Cook, 2011)

ABOUT THE PUBLISHER

Foursquare Missions Press was founded in 1981 with the purpose of providing free gospel literature to the world. To date, this ministry has distributed over 200,000,000 pieces of literature to 115 countries in 60 languages. In August of 2002, the Press established a training and resourcing ministry to children's workers around the world. The Children's Gospel Box ministry assists thousands of children's workers and children annually. Over one million children have been reached and some 17,000 children's workers trained and resourced in 55 nations. Missions Press is a non-profit organization supported by the gifts of its friends.

ABOUT THE CO-AUTHOR

Robert Hunt, MDiv. Talbot Theological Seminary, is the Director of Foursquare Missions Press. For more information of his published works, contact him at **bhunt@foursquare.org**.

Visit our website at:

www.foursquaremissionspress.org